PREDICTIONS

PREDICTIONS

by Joe Fisher
with illustrations compiled
by Peter Commins

A Jonathan-James Book

VNR VAN NOSTRAND REINHOLD COMPANY
NEW YORK   CINCINNATI   TORONTO   LONDON   MELBOURNE

This book is dedicated to Chris Wall and Bridie Mack.

Printed in the United States of America.

Published by Van Nostrand Reinhold Company
A division of Litton Educational Publishing, Inc.
135 West 50th Street, New York, NY 10020, U.S.A.

16 15 14 13 12 11 10 9 8 7 6 5 4 3 2 1

Library of Congress Cataloguing in Publication Data
Fisher, Joe.
    Predictions.
    Includes index.
    1. Prophecies (occult sciences).   2. Prophets.
3. Forecasting.   I. Commins, Peter, joint author.
II. Title.
BF1791.F5   133.3   80-11167

Jonathan-James Books
5 Sultan Street
Toronto, Ontario
Canada M5S 1L6

Edited by David Homel
Designed by Don Fernley

Acknowledgements

For help, advice, support and inspiration in the research, writing and illustration of this book we are grateful, in one way or another, to the following: David Kendall (for creative suggestion and fishing tackle); Angela Burpee (for slaving over hot books into the wee closing hours); Graham Taylor (for Hopping, Graping and setting); Peter Brewster and Gord Stimmell (for paving the way for the author's sabbatical from the *Toronto Sun* newsroom); Richard O'Brien (for a bucketful of research material on the futurists); Jay Bryan (our Montreal correspondent on "Moses" and "Dr. Valium"); John Burns (for Biblical counsel); David Kopman (our one-man African bureau); Barbara and Larry Kopman; Malcolm Fisher (for premonition hunting in London); Cindy Grech and Susan Commins, Cabbagetown's greatest cook.

Our thanks also to Terri Degler of the Canadian Psychic Research Institute; the girls of the *Toronto Sun* library; the staff of the Metro Library, Toronto and the staff of the John P. Robarts Research Library, Toronto; Brenda Brooks of Canadian Press photo services, Toronto; Alan Edmonds; Miki Andres and H. Dingwall Macbeath.

Contents

"We will have colonies on the Moon and on Mars. Between here and the Moon, in all probability, solar receptors to borrow that cup of fire we so dearly need to run our civilizations.

"Space travel will be the greatest joy to come out of future technological society, because it will elevate our spirits as well as lift our heels. THE challenge is immensely exciting and waiting to be taken up, else why all those Star Trekkers, and fans for STAR WARS and CLOSE ENCOUNTERS? The children of our Western civilizations, plus one huge mob in Japan and others all over the world in increasing numbers, are ahead of all the older people in this. THEY sense a cause worth fighting and dying for — not war, but moving through the universe to survive and, Glory Hallelujah, live forever.

Imagine heavens in theological books? No more. We can go somewhere and build a heaven, and live in it, unto a billion generations from this afternoon. We may never reach Andromeda, it's too far away. But we can try."

— Sci-fi specialist Ray Bradbury as told to the author.

Foreword

"O world invisible, we view thee,
  O world intangible, we touch thee,
  O world unknowable, we know thee,
  Unapprehensible, we clutch thee!"

Francis Thompson

We are the hungry ones; we are the ones who want to know what will happen. And so our demand creates the supply. Predictions answer our uncertainties; they nourish our need to know. Yet when we have devoured the predictors' words, we often react like a starving man who complains at being handed stale bread. Our taste is soured even as our hunger is satisfied.

Accordingly, a gentle word of caution: don't be dismayed by the predictors' less-than-optimistic view. From the earliest times, they have never felt obliged to act as comforters. Aside from the occasional obliqueness to save themselves from wrathful rulers, they have always given direct voice to their visions. Why, then, do they so often look on the black side? The best way to answer this question is with another: why are the newspapers packed with unhappy tidings? Good news, unless it's *very* good news, is not considered an event.

Because so many predictions propose an unpalatable upsetting of the way things are, predictors have always suffered persecution and ridicule. Prophets in Roman times who failed to tell the emperors what they wanted to hear were paid in torture or even death. Jesus Christ was scourged for his prophetic ability. Matthew 26 tells us "Then did they spit in his face, and buffeted him; and others smote him with the palms of their hands, saying, Prophesy unto us, thou Christ, Who is he that smote thee?" Scotland's Brahan Seer was thrust head first into a spiked barrel of boiling tar because his words displeased the local nobility and Nostradamus, fearing persecution as a sorcerer, worked at making his prophecies all but unintelligible. More recently, Edgar Cayce was arrested in New York for fortune-telling ("I'm no fortune-teller," he told the judge who acquitted him, "I'm a psychic diagnostician.") and space predictor Immanuel Velikovsky was vilified by some of the world's leading scientists; many scoffed at his ideas without bothering to read his work.

The supernatural having lost many of its terrors, there is a greater tolerance of predictors, and world leaders no longer rush to censure the predictive word. Though we are still awed at times by psychic presentiments, they usually do little more than amuse us. Not that the importance of predictions has dwindled; its emphasis has merely changed. The predictors who hold power today — the futurists — do so because they are valuable to government and commerce and have earned society's respect.

Predictions are drawn from sources as diverse as animal livers, crystal balls, hypnotic trances, planetary positioning and computer gadgetry. But this book is concerned most of all with the predictions themselves. What are they, who made them and why? These pages are both your guide and your grab-bag as we examine predictions through the ages, from the cataleptic utterances of the Biblical seers to the cool projections of today's white collar prophets. Although the predictors can be strikingly different, they are invested with a magnetism common to all. Anyone claiming to unveil the future tugs at our curiosity like a half-heard news flash. Yet there's more to prophecy than the anticipation of what will be. Predictions give our lives dimension and perspective. Predictions enchant us; they convey a sense of infinite chance. They lift us out of the rut and into the ozone.

Since Time holds all secrets, it is the aim of predictions to pry these secrets free. The host of predictions that have come true show this can be done, but exactly *how* it's done defies explanation. Many prophets say past, present and future are one, that they are privileged to read eternity's unbroken scroll both backward and forward. Trapped in linear progression, our aging bodies tell us otherwise. So do the clocks and calendars that regulate our lives and bring the landmark years of 1984 and 2000 closer by the minute.

Because, for the first time in the history of the world, the very survival of civilization is at stake, we don't need predictors to tell us that our generation could be the last. But we *do* want to know the probable future hiding in the thicket of possibilities. As you will see, prophets both ancient and modern agree that we are in for some rude shocks before we bid farewell to the second millennium. While many of the predictions are downright depressing they are not, however, ultimately pessimistic. The consensus is that after trials of war and geological upheaval we will enter a Golden Age of long-lasting peace.

The avid daily consumption of horoscopes and other forecasts about the weather, money markets, fashion trends, horse racing and much more testify to our hankerings. The prophets tap a deeper yearning. There have always been hungry ones, but perhaps we are the hungriest of all. As if the predictors expected this generation's famished condition, they stocked the next twenty years with more predictions than any other period in history.

The prophets have spoken; the table is laid with warnings and promises. Lend a discriminating ear and believe what you will. . . .

I THE CLASSICAL PROPHETS

Predictions know no frontiers in time or space; they slip out of the unimaginably distant past to cross alien cultures and climates. The next four chapters take us from the Middle Eastern deserts to the green hills of Ireland; from an alchemist's study in southern France to the heather of the Scottish Highlands. We begin with the Bible prophets whose sonorous warnings, spanning more than 3,000 years, delight the ear as they chill the heart. Next, Columbcille and Malachy, the saints of old Ireland, predict the course of Irish history and the papal line. Nostradamus, the seer of Salon, relates his visions gathered while "contemplating the remotest of stars." We then examine the peculiar faculty of second sight as it flourished and declined in northern Scotland.

Back we go, back into an insubstantial world of monasticism and mystical insight. From the vaporous past, the predictor's voice rings out strongly, unwaveringly. . . .

The Old and New Testament prophets sent warnings for the ages to come.

1   The Bible

"Wars must come, but the end won't follow immediately.
For nation shall rise against nation and kingdom against
kingdom, and there will be great earthquakes, and famines
in many lands, and epidemics, and terrifying things
happening in the heavens."

Jesus Christ

The Tongues of God

Biblical prophecy is based on one vengeful, immutable law, as clear
and unforgiving as any of the rules that govern the physical world.
"Whoever sins will be punished" stands at the heart of the predictions found in the Bible.

The Hebrew prophets warned again and again that the life of
people and nations today would determine how God would judge
them tomorrow. At the same time, they held out little hope of
changing sinful human nature; they predicted the peoples of the
world would repeat the same mistakes all the way to Armageddon.
Their only consolation was to guarantee salvation for the righteous
(a prediction defying earthly confirmation), and to predict the birth
and death of Jesus Christ. When Christ arrived — and all religious
beliefs aside, his life is historical fact — he not only proved the
predictors right, he also prolonged the prophetic tradition by making
his own forecasts up to and beyond "the time of the end."

Both the Old and New Testaments, spanning 1,600 years of
history, are packed with prophecy from the mouths of men ranging
from shepherds to kings. We are told there was nothing premeditated
about their utterances. Inspiration struck, transforming them into
God's tongues. As the prophet Amos asked rhetorically, "The lion
hath roared — who will not fear? The Lord hath spoken — who
can but prophesy?" (Amos 3:8). It seems the prophets' own thoughts
and feelings were suspended as the Word was received and the
Almighty's message transmitted. Asserts the Apostle Peter: "For the
prophecy came not in old time by the will of man: but holy men
of God spake as they were moved by the Holy Ghost." (2 Peter
1:21).

The early Egyptian prophets made their proclamations in complete darkness. They maintained that inner illumination shone most brightly under such conditions, but their detractors argued that prediction-seekers were more gullible in the dark.

The effects of divine inspiration varied. While Ezekiel sometimes remained in a trance for days, Daniel spoke of his visions throwing him to the ground and even making him physically sick. Theodore H. Robinson, in his book *Prophecy and the Prophets in Ancient Israel*, describes how inspiration might strike an Old Testament seer:

> He might be mingling with the crowd . . . Suddenly something would happen to him. His eyes would become fixed, strange convulsions would seize upon his limbs, the form of his speech would change. Men would recognize that the Spirit had fallen upon him. The fit would pass, and he would tell to those who stood around the things which he had seen and heard. . .

The prophets saw themselves as spiritual ambassadors of Yahweh, which is Hebrew for the "Unnamable," or simply "God." They were vital to their communities' spiritual security and well-being. In the words of Proverbs (29:18), "Where there is no vision, the people perish." Hearing their revelations, people would remember and repeat their words, and later write them down. And so the prophets' collected utterances ended up in the Bible, scattered predictions appearing here and there with little regard for chronological order. All of this makes interpretation a difficult task. Even the devout Martin Luther grumbled about the confusing impression left by the prophets:

> They have a queer way of talking, like people who, instead of proceeding in an orderly manner, ramble off from one thing to the next, so that you cannot make head or tail of them, or see what they are getting at.

There's much, however, that has been clearly presented, and a great deal has come true, often after the passing of many centuries. Some very explicit material about the future of the modern world still waits to be realized. According to responsible interpretation of Bible prophecy, we are on the brink of witnessing the catastrophic fulfillment of the ancient word in the Middle East. Of all the doom that's been shouted down the centuries, this warning of the war to end all wars — "the great winepress of the wrath of God," as the Apostle John calls it — moistens the palms like none other.

The Man of Sorrows
Most Bible predictions can be classified under two general headings: prophecies about Israel and Jerusalem in the years leading up to

and including the life of Christ, and the terrible and magnificent descriptions of the "last days" and Christ's second coming. These awesome accounts of how God will ultimately "destroy them which destroy the earth" (Revelation 11:18) demand to be read with respect once we've seen how accurate the predictions of the Old Testament prophets really were.

In the eighth century before Christ, the prophet Isaiah predicted that Babylon, a second-rate state in his day, would grow into a powerful empire, the "Lady of Kingdoms." The prospects for his people weren't good. He foretold that the soldiers of the emerging empire would overrun the land of Judah, reducing Jerusalem, its capital, to rubble and bearing off the survivors into exile:

> Behold, the days come, that all that is in thine house, and that which thy fathers have laid up in store until this day, shall be carried to Babylon: nothing shall be left, saith the Lord. And of thy sons that shall issue from thee, which thou shalt beget, shall they take away; and they shall be eunuchs in the palace of the king of Babylon.
>
> (Isaiah 39:6,7)

About eighteen years before the Babylonian invasion, the prophet Jeremiah had this to say:

> And this whole land shall be a desolation, and an astonishment; and these nations shall serve the king of Babylon seventy years.
> (Jeremiah 25:11)

Which is just what happened. After seventy years, the Medes and Persians led by Cyrus (whom Isaiah had named 200 years earlier!) diverted the Euphrates River and marched along the watercourse and under the walls to take the mighty capital while Babylon was drunkenly celebrating. Cyrus later released the Israelite prisoners who returned to their homeland to rebuild Jerusalem. Isaiah and Jeremiah went on to say that Babylon, commanding a magnificent site as one of the wonders of the ancient world, would be reduced to "piles of stones," the refuge of jackals and owls, "never to be inhabited again":

> And Babylon shall become heaps, a dwelling place for dragons, an astonishment, and an hissing, without an inhabitant.
> (Jeremiah 51:37)

Centuries after these predictions were logged, Babylon was still

The first recorded economic prediction of all time was made by Joseph around 1600 B.C. Interpreting Pharoah's dreams of seven fat and seven lean cows and seven plump and seven thin ears of corn, he foretold seven years of plenty for Egypt followed by seven years of famine. Joseph advised Pharoah to lay in supplies to withstand the years of drought (Genesis 41:1-36).

inhabited. But soon after the death of Christ, desolation overcame her. Today, there is little evidence of the once-great city and tourists, heading out to the site from nearby Baghdad, are invariably disappointed. "They are shown masses of ruins . . . grey-colored and crumbling, and in no way impressive," wrote André Parrot, head curator of the French National Museums. "The destruction wrought by man has been completed by the ravages of nature. . . No human power can arrest this ceaseless spoilation. It is no longer possible to reconstruct Babylon; her destiny is accomplished."

Daniel, whose predictions often took the form of dramatic visions, foresaw the Medo-Persian empire being crushed by Alexander the Great. He pictured Alexander as a horn on the head of a goat representing the conquering Greeks:

> Therefore the he goat waxed very great: and when he was strong, the great horn was broken; and for it came up four notable ones toward the four winds of heaven.
>
> (Daniel 8:8)

As foretold, Alexander died "when he was strong" in 323 B.C., at the age of thirty-two. Within a few years of his death, his empire had been carved up among four of his generals, the "four notable ones."

The birth of Christ was still centuries away, and many were the triumphs and reversals to be played out on the stage of ancient Israel before the coming of the Messiah. Yet Jesus Christ was already very real to the Old Testament prophets who told, in astonishingly fine detail, the story of the greatest man who ever lived. Professor J.P. Free maintains in his book *Archaeology and Bible History* that there are 332 distinct predictions in Hebrew scriptures that were fulfilled in Jesus. Among the forecasts were the birth of Jesus in Bethlehem, the refusal of many to recognize the Messiah, his triumphant entry into Jerusalem on a donkey, his betrayal for thirty pieces of silver and his crucifixion. Let's take a look at some of them, starting with Christ's nativity. The prophet Micah must have been uncommonly inspired when he declared:

> But thou, Beth-lehem Ephratah, though thou be little among the thousands of Judah, yet out of thee shall he come forth unto me that is to be the ruler in Israel; whose goings forth have been from of old, from everlasting.
>
> (Micah 5:2)

Isaiah, using the affirming prophetic past tense, sadly foretold the scorn, rejection and humiliation Christ was to suffer:

> He is despised and rejected of men; a man of sorrows and acquainted with grief: and we hid as it were our faces from him; he was despised, and we esteemed him not.
>
> (Isaiah 53:3)

Isaiah knew about Jesus' mission as savior and was well-acquainted with the forthcoming miracles:

> . . . he will come and save you. Then the eyes of the blind shall be opened, and the ears of the deaf shall be unstopped. Then shall the lame man leap as an hart, and the tongue of the dumb sing: for in the wilderness shall waters break out, and streams in the desert.
>
> (Isaiah 35:4-6)

Zechariah had a preview of Jesus' tumultuous reception as he entered Jerusalem astride a donkey:

> Rejoice greatly, O daughter of Zion; shout, O daughter of Jerusalem: behold, the King cometh unto thee: he is just, and having salvation; lowly, and riding upon an ass, and upon a colt the foal of an ass.
>
> (Zechariah 9:9)

Christ's betrayal by his disciple Judas Iscariot was to follow soon afterward. As if Jesus were speaking through him, Zechariah named the exact price of Judas' traitorous kiss: "So they weighed for my price thirty pieces of silver." (Zechariah 11:12).

Then came the crucifixion, graphically described by King David more than 1000 years before it happened; before, even, this agonizing method of execution imported by the Romans was known:

> For dogs have encompassed me: the assembly of the wicked have inclosed me; they pierced my hands and my feet. I may tell all my bones: they look and stare upon me. They part my garments among them, and cast lots upon my vesture.
>
> (Psalm 22:16-18)

Jesus Christ was crucified because his contemporaries did not believe his claim that he was the Messiah predicted by the Old Testament prophets. Jesus often referred to these prophecies, hint-ing strongly that his life of tribulation leading to death on the cross was inevitable:

> . . . all things must be fulfilled, which were written in the law of Moses, and in the prophets, and in the psalms, concerning me.
>
> (Luke 24:44)

When Jesus' efforts to win acceptance failed, he warned Jerusalem would fall as a result. The old law of divine judgment was at work again:

> . . . thine enemies shall cast a trench about thee, and compass thee round, and keep thee in on every side, and shall lay thee even with the ground, and thy children within thee: and they shall not leave thee one stone upon another: because thou knewest not the time of thy visitation.
>
> (Luke 19:43,44)

Thirty-seven years after the death of Christ, General Titus and his troops surrounded Jerusalem to put down a revolt by the Jews against their Roman masters. Recording what happened after five months of siege, the historian Josephus wrote: "All the rest of the fortifications encircling the city were so completely leveled with the ground that no one visiting the spot would believe it had once been inhabited." But Jesus had also predicted there would be an opportunity to flee the city, and so there was. The siege was originally mounted in 66 A.D., but the invading forces mysteriously withdrew shortly after. They returned with a vengeance four years later, by which time those who had acted on Jesus' prophecy were well out of danger.

The Time before the End

With the hindsight granted by almost 2000 years of history, we can compare the Old Testament prophets' words about "the time of the end" with those of Jesus and other New Testament prophets. Their predictions tally. The Messiah, they all agree, will return not as a suffering martyr with all the frailties and limitations of mortal man, but as an all-powerful King of the Cosmos, wreaking havoc in judgment of the earth's wayward souls. Many Biblical scholars are sure we are now living in the "last days." And there's no doubt world events are unfolding in a way that could precipitate, in Israel, the legendary Battle of Armageddon.

Centuries before the great exile of the Jewish people more than 1900 years ago, Moses, Ezekiel, Jeremiah, Isaiah and others foretold that the Jews would be thrown out of their homeland to be dogged by privation and persecution. The expression "wandering Jew" was apt:

> And the Lord shall scatter thee among all people, from one end of the earth even unto the other... And among those nations shalt thou find no ease, neither shall the sole of thy foot have rest.
>
> (Deuteronomy 28:64, 65)

As surely as the prophets predicted the Jews' dispersion, they forecast their return. Ezekiel's words were fulfilled on May 14, 1948, when the State of Israel was established in Palestine:

> For I will take you from among the heathen, and gather you out of all countries, and will bring you into your own land.
>
> (Ezekiel 36:24)

Ezekiel went on to say that once back home, the Jews would rework their nation into a land of plenty. Modern Israelis have proved him right. The question is . . . have they unwittingly lit the fuse that will set off Armageddon?

> And they shall say, this land that was desolate is become like the Garden of Eden; and the waste and desolate and ruined cities are become fenced and are inhabited.
>
> (Ezekiel 36:35)

All's well for a while, but in the "latter days" a vast army is assembled "out of the north parts." This geographical location can only be Russia, although Ezekiel, in the language of his time, speaks of "Gog, the land of Magog." And so Gog advances on Israel:

> . . . all thine army, horses and horsemen, all of them clothed with all sorts of armour, even a great company with bucklers and shields, all of them handling swords: Persia, Ethiopia and Libya with them; all of them with shield and helmet.
>
> (Ezekiel 38:4, 5)

Israel is locked in by aggressors, with Russia bearing down from

When Moses assured the Children of Israel they would be provided for during their desert trek from Egypt to the Promised Land, his words were fulfilled in many ways. One of the difficulties solved along the way was the lack of drinking water. Exodus 15:22-25 says the Israelites "went three days in the wilderness and found no water" until they came to Marah where the waters were "bitter." The Bible goes on:

> And the people murmured against Moses, saying, What shall we drink?
> And he cried unto the Lord; and the Lord shewed him a tree which when he had cast into the waters, the waters were made sweet . . .

In the 1940s, Swiss physicist Walter Stark researched the prediction and found a Lebanon pine tree, immersed in the pools found in the Sinai peninsula, neutralizes and absorbs the salts that make the water undrinkable.

the north and the North African states threatening from the south. With the continuing Arab-Israeli tension, the recent forging of alliances between Russia and North African nations and the upheavals in Iran (ancient Persia) which have strengthened that nation's ties with the Soviets, the fulfillment of this prediction is frighteningly possible. Daniel pushes the volatile situation past the point of no return in Chapter 11:40:

> And at the time of the end shall the king of the south push at him [Israel]: and the king of the north shall come against him like a whirlwind, with chariots, and with horsemen, and with many ships. . .

Israel is not the only country invaded; the king of the north "shall stretch forth his hand also upon the countries: and the land of Egypt shall not escape." (Daniel 11:42). Recent conflict, unforeseen a few years ago, between the Soviets and Egyptian premier Anwar Sadat makes this prediction surprisingly significant. But, says Daniel, "tidings out of the east and out of the north" will interfere with the Russians who then "go forth with great fury to destroy." And then something cataclysmic takes place — we can surmise either a horrendous natural disaster or the deadly release of nuclear warheads — to wipe out the Soviet forces. Ezekiel puts it this way:

> At the same time when Gog shall come against the land of Israel . . . there shall be a great shaking in the land . . . and all the men that are upon the face of the earth shall shake at my presence, and the mountains shall be thrown down, and the steep places shall fall, and every wall shall fall to the ground. . . And I will plead against him with pestilence and with blood; and I will rain upon him, and upon his bands, and upon the many people that are with him, an overflowing rain, and great hailstones, fire, and brimstone.
>
> (Ezekiel 38:18-20, 22)

The nuclear holocaust, if that's what Ezekiel is really describing, affects a much greater area than the Middle East. In Chapter 39, verse 6, he adds this postscript:

> And I will send a fire on Magog, and among them that dwell carelessly in the isles.

Yet the annihilation of the Russians is merely a terrifying prelude to the greatest battle the world has ever known. Armageddon is fought out between "the kings of the east," whose troop movements were troubling the Russians, and the western forces led by the "beast" or "Antichrist" who, Bible prophecy tells us, will command unthinkable power. The Antichrist's empire will be maintained largely by his unique ability to make the world a peaceful place to live in. Nevertheless, the beast holds people in awe and subjection:

> . . . and they worshipped the beast, saying, Who is like unto the beast? who is able to make war with him?
>
> (Revelation 13:4)

Never will the world have known such a dominating figure. For forty-two months, says Revelation, the beast will control the earth. The apostle John, the author of Revelation, explains the economic vice-grip the beast has on each individual:

> And he causeth all, both small and great, rich and poor, free and bond, to receive a mark in their right hand, or in their

Israeli tanks near the Golan Heights. Is the Arab-Israeli conflict the prelude to Armageddon?

foreheads: And that no man might buy or sell, save he that had the mark, or the name of the beast, or the number of his name . . . it is the number of a man; and his number is Six hundred threescore and six.

(Revelation 13:16-18)

But in the end, even the beast cannot keep the peace. His supremacy is challenged by "the king of the east" (China and her allies) who masses an army of 200 million and advances across the dry riverbed of the Euphrates:

And the four angels were loosed, which were prepared for an hour, and a day, and a month, and a year, for to slay the third part of men. And the number of the army of the horsemen were two hundred thousand thousand: and I heard the number of them.

(Revelation 9:15, 16)

Some of China's militia of millions, frighteningly redolent of the forces of the "Kings of the East."

Two hundred million troops is no longer as unlikely as it was at the time the prediction was made. In China alone, in 1961, there were an estimated 200,000,000 armed and organized militiamen, according to an Associated Press release. And so the dreaded confrontation takes place: East against West.

> And he gathered them together into a place called in the Hebrew tongue Armageddon. And there were voices, and thunders, and lightnings; and there was a great earthquake, such as was not since men were upon the earth, so mighty an earthquake, and so great. And every island fled away, and the mountains were not found. And there fell upon men a great hail out of heaven, every stone about the weight of a talent: and men blasphemed God because of the plague of the hail; for the plague thereof was exceeding great.
>
> (Revelation 16:16, 18, 20-1)

Armageddon is located on the great plain of Jezreel which runs southeast from the Israeli port of Haifa. So great is the carnage in this most terrible of all confrontations that Revelation 14:20 describes blood flowing out in a stream "200 miles long and high as a horse's bridle." In a passage that sounds very much like the effects of radiation, Zechariah talks about the "plague wherewith the Lord will smite all the people that have fought against Jerusalem." He says:

> Their flesh shall consume away while they stand upon their feet, and their eyes shall consume away in their holes, and their tongue shall consume away in their mouth.
>
> (Zechariah 14:12)

Isaiah sums up by saying "the earth shall reel to and fro like a drunkard" as "the inhabitants of the earth are burned and few men are left." The end of the world, it appears, is at hand. But as the armies compete to inflict the greatest destruction, the longed-for second coming of Christ will prevent the liquidation of mankind. As Jesus explained to his disciples:

> And except those days should be shortened, there should no flesh be saved: but for the elect's sake those days shall be shortened.
>
> (Matthew 24:22)

Judgment will be meted out; the faithful will be assigned positions of responsibility in the new order and the survivors will finally understand the futility of their willfulness:

> And he shall judge among many people, and rebuke strong nations afar off; and they shall beat their swords into plow shares, and their spears into pruninghooks: nation shall not lift up a sword against nation, neither shall they learn war any more.
>
> (Micah 4:3)

Peace at last! This is how Isaiah describes life in the blessed age that succeeds the holocaust:

Ezekiel describes Israel's attackers as "clothed with all sorts of armour . . . all . . . handling swords."

> And they shall build houses, and inhabit them; and they shall plant vineyards, and eat the fruit of them. . . They shall not labour in vain, nor bring forth for trouble. . . The wolf and the lamb shall feed together, and the lion shall eat straw like the

bullock. . . They shall not hurt nor destroy in all my holy mountain, saith the Lord.

But first we must be refined by fire, and according to the Bible, the fire will burn at its hottest after the warning signs of "wars and rumours of wars," intense earthquake activity, widespread epidemics, famine, a glut of false religions and a prevailing atmosphere of fear and lawlessness. Is there not an unmistakable echo here of life in the twentieth century? Jesus gave the warning of warnings in Mark 13:8:

> For nation shall rise against nation, and kingdom against kingdom: and there shall be earthquakes in divers places, and there shall be famines and troubles: and these are the beginnings of sorrows.

Jesus also spoke of false prophets appearing to "deceive many. And because iniquity shall abound, the love of many shall wax cold." (Matthew 24:11, 12). Again, Jesus predicted:

Earthquakes — the shape of things to come, according to the Bible. The Golden State freeway near Los Angeles after the quake of '71.

Shaping up to be one of the most accurate nineteenth century predictions is Charles Richet's forecast that Russia and the United States will be the two most powerful nations in 1992 with a "combined population . . . around 600 million, which will be much larger than that of all Europe." (*In 100 Years,* by Charles Richet, published in 1892)

And there shall be signs in the sun, and in the moon, and in the stars; and upon the earth distress of nations, with perplexity; the sea and the waves roaring; men's hearts failing them for fear, and for looking after those things which are coming on the earth: for the powers of heaven shall be shaken.

(Luke 21:25, 26)

After these dramatic portents, we're told the end will come "as travail upon a woman with child" (I Thessalonians 5:3). And as horrible as this end will be, out of it will come a beginning, "a new heaven and a new earth," according to Revelation 21:1:

And God shall wipe away all tears from their eyes; and there shall be no more death, neither sorrow, nor crying, neither shall there be any more pain: for the former things are passed away.

(Revelation 21:4)

Bible chronology appears to place us near the winding up of the long preparatory phase culminating in the "time of the end." After two world wars, global tension remains. Crime, as well as the incidence of earthquakes and volcanic activity, is on the increase. Countless gurus and outlandish religions have emerged to answer man's need to believe in something greater than himself. All this points to the age before Armageddon in the timetable of events projected by the Bible predictors.

So we're left listening helplessly as the global timebomb ticks on. Or are we? Not according to Rabbi Edgar Magnin of Los Angeles who, in a 1959 lecture entitled *The Voice of Prophecy in this Satellite Age,* interpreted the prophets' words to mean there *is* still hope for the individual who lives the best way he knows how. Formal lip service will not save us, said Magnin. Nor will ritual or organization or churches and synagogues laid end to end around the globe. "Sisterhoods and brotherhoods and more rabbis and ministers and priests will not save us," he went on, "any more than more universities and more professors and more libraries. Nothing will save us but our own souls."

Certainly, the message of the prophets is unequivocal. With one voice, they warn that we stand before a God of judgment, that our misdeeds will be remembered and that the Almighty will mercilessly punish the evil and unfaithful as he saves the righteous. "Go ahead," the prophets seem to say. "Do as you wish. But remember this: as you do now, so will your deeds be weighed later. And if you've pandered to your lower, selfish self — beware!"

There's no need to debate the different religious philosophies that either absorb or reject the teachings of the Old and New Testaments. We would say one thing only: the Bible predictors cried out in the wilderness about the first coming of Christ — their words shouldn't be shrugged off so thoughtlessly a second time.

The Ardmore Round Tower, County Waterford, in the land of St. Columbcille and St. Malachy.

2 The Irish Saints

"For the great Gaels of Ireland
Are the men that God made mad. . ."

G.K. Chesterton

Picture rough seas, rugged headlands, green hills and lonely dwellings. Picture piles of peat and pooks of hay, the rising of blue turf smoke, cowled monks chanting at vespers. Picture an Ireland long before the interference of the English, long before industrialization, fighting in the streets and urban assassinations, long before the poet William Butler Yeats lamented "Romantic Ireland's dead and gone." This was the Emerald Isle of St. Columbcille and St. Malachy, the greatest of Irish prophets, who wrote about their respective preoccupations — the Irish nation and the papacy — with fertile foreboding.

St. Columbcille, who lived in the sixth century, foretold the painful progress of Ireland's history. And St. Malachy, a twelfth century archbishop, penned 112 Latin mottos labeling every pope until the destruction of Rome when "the awful judge will judge the people." Ominously, there are just two more popes left on Malachy's list.

The Travail of Eire
St. Columbcille was born in County Donegal in 522 and grew up to earn himself an impressive reputation as a monastic founder. The suffix "cille" (meaning a monastic cell or church) was added to his name to distinguish him from the numerous other Columbas of old Ireland. We know the Saint lived to be seventy-five years old — a very advanced age for those exacting, if romantic, days — and that at the age of forty-one he set sail with twelve disciples for Britain, settling on the island of Iona. There he built a monastery and wrote countless volumes of religious and prophetic tracts, psalms, hymns and poems. Tradition holds that, in the course of a thirty-four year

Years before the Spanish invasion of Mexico, predictions abounded among the Indians that bearded men from across the sea would overrun the ancient Aztec empire. Seers interpreted a famine, an eclipse, an earthquake and a lingering comet as signs that the end of their civilization was imminent.

In 1508, King Montezuma had a vision of something never before seen in the Americas: men advancing astride animals that he called deer. Around the same time, Paranazin, Montezuma's sister, fell into a trance and told of seeing great ships from a far country bearing armed invaders who carried banners and wore strange "caskets" on their heads. They would, she predicted, become masters of the Aztec lands.

In 1519, the prophecies were fulfilled when Hernando Cortes led his ruthless horse-soldiers into Mexico.

pilgrimage, he made missionary journeys throughout Scotland, the isles of the Hebrides, Orkneys, Shetlands, Faroes and even Iceland.

But it was his beloved Ireland, faced with oncoming centuries of strife and subjection, that concerned St. Columbcille the prophet. The future appeared particularly bleak when compared to the peaceful present. In the opening stanza of the poem-prophecy *Eire this Night*, he describes the times in which he lived:

> How prosperous Eire is this night!
> Her immense substance is free from taxation
> Her princes are hospitable, her palaces are full,
> Her people numerous, and her crops productive.

But even as he writes, there's menace in the air:

> Though this Eire is so prosperous this night,
> A time will come when she will be reduced to destitution;
> A powerful force of strangers will invade her,
> From Lochlan of the sea-faring Galls.

St. Columbcille is referring to the marauding Vikings who were to pillage and destroy churches and monasteries along the Irish coast in the eighth, ninth and tenth centuries. Though the Vikings were curbed by the second half of the tenth century, an Anglo-Norman invasion was to follow in 1169. St. Columbcille saw this most clearly:

> Another race of invaders will come hither across the seas,
> Their number shall be few, though their power prove great,
> Six hundred years and ninety more in full,
> Shall they impose their tributes upon us.

> They will take possession of a portion of Ireland,
> Their progress shall be but slow in the beginning;
> But they will forcibly extend their supremacy,
> With a lubriciousness similar to that of a mist stealing upon a headland.

While St. Columbcille under-estimated the duration of the English presence, he was correct in saying the invaders, numbering only 600 in the beginning, would be slow to impress their superiority. For some time, they restricted themselves to a corner of Ireland known as "The English Pale." Not until the Tudor kings and queens acceded to the English throne was Ireland truly conquered. As John Richard Green writes in *A Short History of the English People*, every vestige of the old Celtic constitution was rejected as "barbarous" and the tribal authority of the chiefs taken from them by law. "The evicted natives," noted Green, "withdrew sullenly to the lands which had been left them by the spoiler; but all faith in English justice had been torn from the minds of the Irishry, and the seed had been sown of that fatal harvest of distrust and disaffection, which was to be reaped through tyranny and massacre in the age to come."

St. Columbcille described the English offensive this way:

> They will persecute the Gaels with galling ferocity;
> Their petitions for restitution will be disregarded.

The Irish rebellion of 1641 led to a brutal scourging under the heel of Oliver Cromwell and his Parliamentarian forces. This was Green's "tyranny and massacre" that the Saint predicted:

> An uninterrupted course of warfare will mark their career
> While their keen-edged swords shall be ever reeking with blood;
> Fire, robbery, and every species of infliction will prevail,
> They will persecute the Gael into exile.

St. Columbcille foresaw not only military subjection but cultural domination. The Irish were to speak the hated and less poetic English tongue, their churches were to be commandeered by Protestants and, later, they were to be confronted by the bewitching imposition of "fiery chariots" — the railway:

> An uncultivated language will be found in every person's mouth,
> Proud abbots will rule over every sanctified church:

"The destiny of Ireland is to become an English sheep walk and cattle pasture."
— Karl Marx

The railway, introduced by the English, which was to bewitch the Irish with "druidical deception."

Gregory Rasputin's death and his nation's future were inseparable.

The "mad monk" of Russia wrote a letter which was shown to the Tsarina soon after it was composed. In it was the prediction that he would be murdered by January 1, 1917. The letter also said that should he die at the hands of the peasantry, Russia would have a prosperous monarchy for centuries. But if he was killed by the "boyars" (the aristocracy), the Tsar and his family would die within two years and the nobility would be no more.

On the night of December 29, 1916, Rasputin was murdered by Prince Yussupov who gave him cakes and wine laced with cyanide, shot him twice, bashed him with an iron bar and dropped him into a river through a hole in the ice. The Revolution came the following year and the Tsar and his family were imprisoned before being executed on July 16, 1918. The Russian aristocracy, of course, has since been wiped out.

In both north and south iron wheels shall support
Fiery chariots, which shall resemble druidical deception.

The great potato famine of 1845-50 and an ensuing fever epidemic killed one million Irish and encouraged the emigration to Britain, America, Canada and Australia of another million. Again, St. Columbcille was there first. "Dearth will become oppressive throughout the land," he wrote. "Plague will consume the powerful as well as the weak." And then:

The pure fair Gael will fly away
Into exile into both the eastern and western regions of the world.

Home Rule for Ireland (or at least for Southern Ireland) wasn't to become a reality until the Anglo-Irish Treaty of 1921 established the Irish Free State. Since then, of course, unresolved arguments in Northern Ireland have provoked violent reactions against the old enemy. St. Columbcille, confident the "false-hearted Galls" would suffer dearly for their inflictions, predicted England's enemies would be "aroused into activity" to vanquish the oppressors of the Irish in a sea battle. The aftermath of this defeat is grim indeed for the English:

The Saxons afterwards shall dwindle down into a disreputable people,
And every obstacle shall be opposed to their future prosperity:
Because they did not observe justice and rectitude,
They shall be for ever after deprived of power!

The English will know their downfall is imminent when they have been handed three warnings:

Three warnings shall be given them before their final fall,
The burning of the Tower of the great kings,
The conflagration of the Dockyard of the Galls,
And the burning of the Treasury where gold is deposited.

If we accept bomb damage sustained in World War Two as "burning" and "conflagration," then the first two warnings have already been given. The Tower of London went up in smoke after German air raids scored fifteen direct hits, and fire raged through the dockland after a particularly devastating bombing in September, 1940. Fire has yet to sweep through the Bank of England for warning

The strife predicted by St. Columbcille continues to divide the Irish nation.

Prince Jayabhaya of Java predicted in the twelfth century that Indonesia would one day attain permanent independence after falling under the rule of a yellow race. When the Japanese occupied the islands in World War Two, Indonesians recalled the prophecy and looked for their freedom to follow. It did. Independence was declared on August 17, 1945 and, after four and a half years of resistance from Dutch colonialists, was established in 1950.

number three. Considering current times, this final warning might take the form of IRA bombings in the heart of London.

Turning to the fate of his own country, St. Columbcille enthused about a new prosperous Ireland: "Great shall be her renown and her power." But he invoked an ancient Irish tradition in saying the nation is destined in the end to be drowned:

> . . . seven years before the last day,
> The sea shall submerge Eirin by one inundation.

John O'Connell in his *Poem on Ireland* explained that God had pledged such a merciful end to spare the Irish the lies of the Antichrist and the horrors of Armageddon:

> Lest the deceptions, snares and danger
> Of Antichrist should fall upon the Irish;
> He promised to send a deluge over Ireland,
> Seven years previous to the burning of the spheres.

Like many prophets, St. Columbcille brooded darkly about the future of man in much of his writing. Devout as he was, he couldn't foresee religious principles chastening the generations to come. In his quaint, archaic way, he divined the coming of the permissive age. "Young women will become unblushing," he said. "There shall be no standard by which morals may be regulated, and marriages will be solemnized without witnesses." Indeed, St. Columbcille sounds thoroughly grateful to have been born in the sixth century when man feared God and Ireland was strong in her isolation. He had no desire to live forever; his foresight told him that "more unjust and iniquitous shall be every succeeding race of man!"

Saint Peter's Succession

Some 550 years after the death of St. Columbcille, the Archbishop of Armagh, Malachy O'Morgair (later to be canonized as St. Malachy), had visions of future popes. To identify each man in the long line of pontiffs succeeding the pope of his day, Innocent II, he jotted down 112 inscriptions, most of them no longer than a couple of words. Malachy's amazing insight is remarked upon by his friend and biographer, St. Bernard of Clairvaux, who tells us that Malachy even foretold the day and hour of his own death in 1148. Strange, then, that St. Bernard makes no mention of the papal prophecies in his biography. Actually, the inscriptions which identified each of St. Peter's successors until the papacy comes to an end weren't published until 1595, when a Benedictine historian named Arnold Wion discovered and casually made the prophecies public. Wion explained that the manuscript was given to Pope Innocent II (a claim corroborated by Abbé Cucherat who wrote that Malachy composed his prophecies while on a visit to Rome in 1139-40) and that the pontiff consigned the work to the Vatican archives. Until Wion's chance find, it had languished there for more than 400 years. This unusual explanation led some scholars to believe the manuscript to be a forgery, but others, weightier in number and reputation, have since accepted Malachy's prophecies as genuine. Certainly, the high accuracy rate of St. Malachy's epithets since the 1595 discovery undermines the forgery theory. Let's examine some of these more recent examples:

- Alexander VII (1655-67) . . . His family crest showed three hills under the watchful light of a star. *"Montium custos"* or "guardian of the hills," said Malachy.
- Clement XIII (1758-69) . . . He was stationed in Umbria before becoming pope. Umbria's symbol is a rose. Malachy put the two together, writing *"rosa Umbriae"* or "rose of Umbria."
- Clement XIV (1769-75) . . . This pope's family shield depicted a running bear. *"Ursus velox,"* wrote Malachy, or "swift bear."
- Pius VI (1775-99) . . . Unseated by the French Revolution, he spent the rest of his life wandering as a fugitive. Malachy's motto for him was *"peregrinus apostolicus"* or "apostolic wanderer."
- Gregory XVI (1831-46) . . . Hailing from an order in Etruria, he sponsored archaeological research on the ancient baths of that province. *"De balneis Etruriae"* or "from the baths of Etruria" was Malachy's appellation.

So far, the most accurate prophecy about the popes of this century was the description of Benedict XV: *"religio depopulata"* or "religion depopulated." While Malachy's puzzled readers were wondering how this pontiff could possibly fit the severity of his inscription, World War One broke out. The message for the one hundred and fourth pope was all too clear. His reign, which lasted from 1914 until 1922, saw the slaying of millions of Christians on European battlefields and, after the Russian Revolution of 1917, the isolation of some 200 million more faithful from the Roman Catholic fold.

Malachy's predictions have maintained their reputation for accuracy with the last few popes. John XXIII (1958-63) was called *"pastor et nauta"* or "shepherd and sailor." "Shepherd" is clear enough; it applies to the keeper of a flock that follows "The Good Shepherd." Pope John was a well-loved leader, and he used his shepherding qualities to subtly change the course of the Roman Catholic Church. The "sailor" may refer to his style of leadership at the helm of the Vatican, or it may be a simple reference to his maritime associations as Patriarch of Venice.

St. Malachy chose *"flors florum"* ("flower of flowers") for Pope Paul VI, and the pope carried, appropriately enough, the *fleur-de-lys* on his coat of arms. Next came the thirty-three day reign of Pope John Paul I on whom the Saint, in his sometimes ambiguous Latin, bestowed *"de medietate lunae,"* which could mean either "from the half moon" or "of the middle moon." John Paul, elected to lead the world's 600 million Catholics on August 26, 1978, died suddenly on September 28 that same year, making his tenure as brief as Malachy had suggested more than 900 years before. The pope's death occured roughly in the middle of the lunar month, between the full moons of September 16 and October 16.

Interpreters are still scratching their heads over the significance of *"de labore solis,"* St. Malachy's epithet for Pope John Paul II. "From the sun's labor," reads the translation. Some commentators have been tempted to speculate on a connection with solar energy

John Paul I's thirty-three day reign was between two full moons, or *"de medietate lunae,"* as Malachy described it.

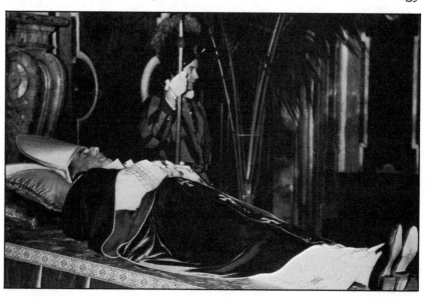

but the link, at best, is tenuous. Time should uncork the mystery.

What is St. Malachy forecasting for the future? The next pope has the motto *"Gloria olivae,"* or "glory of the olive," which suggests a peacemaking role. But according to Malachy, any peace secured in the reign of the second-to-last pope will be short-lived. *"Petrus Romanus,"* or "Peter of Rome," is the last of the predicted popes. After this inscription, Malachy adds a telling postscript for the first and only time:

> In the final persecution of the Holy Roman Church, there shall sit Peter of Rome, who shall feed the sheep among great tribulations. When these have passed, the City of the Seven Hills will be destroyed and the dreadful judge will judge the people.

St. Malachy's message couldn't be clearer. Peter of Rome is the pope of the apocalypse, the pope of the final judgment whose leadership will nourish the faithful in the last days before Rome is brought crashing to the ground. If the present pontiff and his two successors each reigned for an average term of seven years, St. Malachy's prophecies would put the end of the papacy around the year 2000 — a prediction neatly coinciding with other prophets' woebegone scenarios of the century in shutdown.

The "pig half-man . . . Brute beasts will be heard to speak." With these words, Nostradamus characterized air warfare three and a half centuries before the fact.

3 Nostradamus

"Hidden prophecies come by the subtle spirit of fire,
sometimes through the understanding being disturbed in
contemplating the remotest of stars . . ."

Nostradamus

The Harsh Muse

To endeavor to understand prophetic inspiration and its transmutation into words is like trying to catch the wind. For our consideration — but hardly for our enlightenment — Nostradamus, the crown prince of prophecy, attempts to explain the process in opening his doom-laden *Centuries*:

> Sitting at night in my secret study
> Alone, resting on the brass stool,
> A slender flame leaps out of the solitude
> Making me pronounce that which is not in vain.

The "flame" or "subtle spirit of fire" is clearly the cryptic connection between the great Unknown and the seer's otherworldly insights. "It is much like seeing in a burning mirror, with clouded vision," he wrote. "The human understanding, being created intellectually, cannot see hidden things unless aided by the voice coming from limbo via the thin flame, showing in what direction future events incline."

According to Nostradamus, events incline at a steep angle of shock, although he never appears to have been awe-struck, or even mildly surprised, by his visions. Barely have the *Centuries* been introduced when horror takes over. Immediately there's a monarch "who will not have peace," there's "great fighting" and there are people being "plunged into death." For Michel Nostradamus, the bearded Jewish doctor from Salon in the south of France, did not always see what we would have liked him to see. Charming though the evocative picture language of his prophecies may be, his future of the world is one long litany of plague, famine, war and disaster.

Many of his predictions have already come true. Certainly the post-war generations can attest to the accuracy of his primitive descriptions of nuclear warfare. Mercifully, however, Nostradamus does see an end at last to the slaughter and catastrophe. He predicts that shortly after June 21, 2002, there will be "a new king annointed who for a long time shall pacify the earth." But more about that later.

Nostradamus, arguably the greatest predictor of all time, was born on December 14, 1503 in St. Remy in Southern France, the son of a notary public and the eldest of five brothers. By the time he was nine years old his parents, living in an age that demanded religious conformity, had converted from Judaism to Catholicism, and Nostradamus was raised as a Christian. He was a brilliant child who developed an early interest in astrology and astronomy, and his classmates even nicknamed him "the little astrologer."

While studying humanities at Avignon University, he taught his fellow students that the earth was round and circled, along with the other planets, around the sun — a revolutionary statement for his day, considering that nearly one hundred years later, Galileo was persecuted for holding the same belief. He moved on to study medicine at Montpellier University and graduated with a doctorate. His unorthodox yet often successful remedies earned him recognition during the plague years that followed.

In 1534, he married a young girl "of high estate, very beautiful and admirable." She bore him two sons before a fresh outbreak of the plague, against which Nostradamus had battled so valiantly, killed her and her children. Nostradamus, grief-stricken, set off on eight years of wandering through France, Italy and Sicily, stopping only to work as a physician.

It was during these itinerant years that he began to realize his prophetic gifts. A story from his journey through Italy tells how he fell on his knees before a young Franciscan monk named Felix Peretti, addressing him as "Your Holiness." This prompted a bemused reaction from those who witnessed the event, since they knew the monk was a former swineherd of humble parents. Yet in time, this same lowly monk became Cardinal of Montalto and in 1585 — nineteen years after the death of Nostradamus — he was proclaimed Pope Sixtus V.

Another travel story has Nostradamus lodging at the Lorraine castle of the Lord of Florinville, a skeptic bent on proving the fallibility of Nostradamus' claim to visionary powers. While out walking one day, the nobleman asked Nostradamus to prophesy the fate of two barnyard pigs, one white, the other black. Nostradamus replied that the noble would eat the black one and a wolf would devour the white one. Secretly, the Lord went to his cook and ordered him to kill the white pig and serve it for supper. The cook killed and prepared the pig, but as the animal lay on the spit ready for roasting, a wolf cub captured by the nobleman's men slunk into the kitchen while the cook was away and began eating the pig. Too late, the cook discovered what had happened. Fearing his master's anger, he hastily killed, roasted and served the black pig at the Lord's table. The Lord gloated over Nostradamus' undoing, telling him with great satisfaction that the white pig was before them; how, then, could a wolf have devoured the animal? On the contrary, Nostradamus replied; events had unfolded just as he said they would. So the nobleman ordered the cook to bring in the pig, but instead of proving his guest wrong, he managed only to squeeze a contrite confession from his servant, vindicating the prediction.

As well as healing the sick, Nostradamus the physician concocted health potions and prepared beauty creams in the finest tradition of alchemists. In 1547 he married again, this time in the Provencal town of Salon. There he stayed on to write the 942 verses of the *Centuries* that made him famous throughout Europe and the world. Before long, so many kings, nobles, prelates and intellectuals beat a path to his door that Jean Aymes de Chavigny, the student, disciple and biographer of the great man, wrote, "Those who came to France sought Nostradamus as the only thing to be seen there."

Though his visions have enthralled millions, Nostradamus was not someone who would stand out in a crowd. "He was a little under medium height, of robust body, nimble and vigorous," wrote de Chavigny. "He had a large forehead, a straight and even nose, grey eyes which were generally pleasant but which blazed when he was angry and a visage both severe and smiling. . . By nature he was taciturn, thinking much and saying little, though speaking well in the proper time and place: for the rest, vigilant, prompt and impetuous, prone to anger, patient in labor."

Patiently accomplished though his work may have been, it was also charged with passion. Chavigny tells us that Nostradamus, who claimed his prophetic gift was hereditary, spent half his nights in visionary dreams, and that he received and wrote his *Centuries* "in a state of ecstasy, rapt in a new madness."

The "voices" of Joan of Arc (1412-1431) kept her supplied with a steady stream of prophecies. She successfully predicted her wounding by an arrow, the brevity of her mission ("I have so little time," she would say. "One year and a little more.") and French victories over the English. One of St. Joan's first recorded prophecies was made outside the castle of Chinon as she answered a man who cursed at her. "In God's name you swear, and you so near death?" was Joan's reply. Within the hour, the man drowned after falling into the castle moat.

Prophecy in Code

Nostradamus prepared his prophecies in quatrains, or four-line verses, which were grouped together in "centuries," or groups of one hundred. He wrote ten centuries, as well as a few other fragmentary stanzas, but Century Seven, for reasons unknown, contains only forty-two quatrains. The quatrains don't follow a chronological pattern, but every so often clusters of two or three can be read in sequence. Much of what he wrote is hard to understand, some is indecipherable and most is open to wide-ranging interpretation. But after exploring the labyrinth of verses made even more confusing by anagrams, mystery names and deliberately obscure imagery, it *is* still possible to pinpoint predictions of remarkable accuracy and determine something of the future according to Nostradamus.

Like all predictors living in Christendom, he was afraid of being persecuted as a sorcerer. He wrote in an epistle to Henry II of France, "If I had wanted to date each quatrain I could have done so. But this . . . was not to be done . . . lest calumniators be furnished with an opportunity to injure me." But he did claim elsewhere that his tortuous prophecies have "but one sense and only one meaning."

His first book of prophecies, comprising 354 quatrains and dedicated to his infant son, César, appeared in March, 1555. "It is possible, my son," wrote Nostradamus in the preface, "that some will raise their eyebrows at seeing such a vast extent of time and treatment of everything under the moon that will happen throughout the earth. But if you attain the natural span of human life, you will come to see, under your own native skies, the fulfillment of future events that I have foreseen."

And so it was, before César was five years older, that one of his father's most riveting quatrains had come true. Nostradamus had written in Century 1.35:

> The young lion shall overcome the old,
> On the field of battle in single combat:
> In a cage of gold he will pierce his eyes,
> Two wounds one, then die a cruel death.

In the summer of 1559, French royalty was celebrating a double marriage with a three-day jousting tournament. King Henry the Second, one of the principal combatants, distinguished himself with prowess and skill until the evening of the third day when he rode against "the young lion," Montgomery, captain of his Scottish guard. After failing to unseat Montgomery in the first bout, the King insisted they tilt again. Montgomery was reluctant but the "old lion" wouldn't take no for an answer. They charged and their lances missed. But in the third encounter both men made contact; their lances splintered and Montgomery failed to drop his shaft in time. The jagged point of his lance broke through the King's visor (his "cage of gold"), piercing his eye. Another splinter is said to have entered his throat, making "two wounds one." Henry II, who had earlier summoned Nostradamus to his court to discuss his newly-published *Centuries*, survived the rudimentary skills of the best surgeons in the land for another ten days before dying "a cruel death."

The fulfillment of this prediction firmly established Nostradamus' reputation and set people scouring the rest of his *Centuries* for shreds of truth. But fearing persecution as a sorcerer and heretic, the prophet covered his tracks so well that few of his would-be interpreters could make any sense of his writings. Even without the camouflage, however, the predicted events were often too bizarre to be imagined with any seriousness. Who among his contemporaries, for example, could have conceived of an overthrow as dramatic as the French Revolution?

With the passing of time, we have come to realize that Nostradamus accurately forecast a host of happenings, ranging from an English naval blitz on Spanish treasure ships at Cadiz to Adolf Hitler's machinations of war; from the invention of the submarine, airplane and Montgolfier balloon to the era of space stations and nuclear war.

In June, 1596 — thirty years after Nostradamus' death — the English naval commanders Essex, Howard and Raleigh unleashed a surprise attack on Cadiz where Spanish galleons lay stocked with treasure, having just dropped anchor after a seven month voyage from South America. Thirteen Spanish warships and forty galleons were destroyed. The water around Cadiz harbor, sheltered by a long lip of land, resembles a lake. Nostradamus put it this way in Century 8.94:

> Before the lake where most treasure was cast,
> Of seven months and its host discomforted,
> The Spaniards will be plundered by the Albions,
> By delaying, loss in giving the conflict.

The elderly and infirm Cardinal Richelieu of France, who died on December 4, 1642, not only lost his office in his last days but was also deprived of command of the army. He was betrayed by

Most unappetizingly, writer Jacques Cazotte (1720-1792) predicted at a Paris dinner party in 1788 that should any of the guests escape the scaffold, they would either commit suicide or die at the hands of the mob. The guests, unaware the French Revolution was imminent, clinked their glasses and laughed at him. But within six years all the diners suffered the end Cazotte had foretold.

his protege, twenty-year-old Cinq Mars. Again, Nostradamus was there before it happened:

Old Cardinal by the young man deceived,
Will see himself disarmed out of his charge.

(8.68)

An avowed monarchist, Nostradamus was horrified by the vision he had of the French Revolution, or the "Vulgar Advent" as he called it. Most of all, he hated the thought of Napoleon. The French Emperor, in the guise of "Pau, nay, loron," is the subject of Century 8.1:

Pau, nay, loron will be more fire than blood,
To swim in praise, the great one to flee on the confluence of
    waters,

One of the few portraits of Michel Nostradamus.

The agassas shall be refused entry,
Most villainous, the Durance will hold them imprisoned.

This quatrain shows exactly how labyrinthine Nostradamus' writing can be. He refers to Napoleon as "more fire than blood," more of a warrior (fire) than a nobleman (blood). The Emperor's famous flight from Elba is described, as well as his imprisonment of Popes Pius VI and Pius VII. How do we know? "Agassas" is Greek for "magpie," or *pie* as the French say. *Pie*, strangely enough, also means pious, or Pius — the two imprisoned popes. Both unfortunate pontiffs were held in southeastern France, a region crossed by the Durance River.

As Nostradamus viewed Napoleon and the French Revolution with distaste, so did he cringe at the execution of England's Charles I, which was to take place in 1649. "The English Parliament will

Cardinal Richelieu was indeed stripped of his powers before his death in 1642, as Nostradamus had foretold.

Marie-Josephe Rose Tascher de la Pagerie was much amused by a Negro seeress' prediction that she would one day become queen. She was living on the island of Martinique at the time and was about to be married at sixteen to a minor French officer, Beauharnais. But it so happened that Beauharnais was guillotined in the French Reign of Terror and Marie-Josephe, lucky to survive, went on to marry another officer, Bonaparte. When Napoleon became emperor, she became empress of France as well as his Josephine.

put to death their king" (9.49), he wrote, foreseeing the Great Fire of London as a vengeful act of God against Cromwell and his band of king-killers:

> The blood of the just will complain to London,
> Burnt by fireballs at twenty three the sixes,
> The ancient lady shall fall from her high place,
> Of the same sect many will be destroyed.
>
> (2.51)

Not only did Nostradamus predict the date of the fire (1666) but he also spoke of the destruction of St. Paul's Church on whose site had once stood the ancient temple of Diana.

Distant Battles

Perhaps the most chilling of the fulfilled quatrains are those concerning Adolf Hitler, or "Hister" as Nostradamus called him. Hister is also an archaic name for the River Danube, so the appellation did double duty for the prophet. There are several telling Hister quatrains; the most appropriately sinister of all is Century 5.29:

> Liberty shall not be recovered,
> A black, fierce and wicked villain shall occupy it,
> When the material of the bridge is completed,
> The republic of Venice shall be annoyed by Hister.

The first two lines are obvious. The second two relate to the pontoon bridge thrown across the Danube from Rumania to Bulgaria. On February 21, 1941, the New York Herald Tribune ran a headline declaring: "SOFIA REPORTS NAZI BRIDGE OVER DANUBE." Within a month, there were dispatches testifying to the German infiltration of the "Republic of Venice," standing for Italy. Even sticklers who insist on meticulous wording can't fault the prophet on this one. It would have been easier, if not quite exact, for him to use the word "built" rather than "when the material of the bridge is completed." We can only assume he was taking careful note that the bridge was of makeshift pontoon construction!

Still on World War Two, Nostradamus wrote:

> The machines of flying fire
> Will come to trouble the great commander of the besieged:
> Inside there will be such sedition
> That the overthrown will be in despair.
>
> (6.34)

Nostradamus was preoccupied by the travail France would pass through during the First and Second World Wars.

This stanza predicts the flame-throwing tanks that trundled across France to conquer Paris. That Paris was also weakened by seditious working from within is historical fact. Citizens of the city betrayed each other as the forces of Marshall Pétain and the Partisans struggled for control.

"Look to Africa," declared Jamaican Marcus Garvey, founder of the visionary Rastafarian movement. "Where a black king shall be crowned, for the day of deliverance is near."

This prophecy was fulfilled in 1930 with the coronation of Haile Selassie — Prince Ras Tafari — as emperor of Ethiopia. Selassie died in 1975, but the Rastafarian vision of a free Africa and the liberation of all black people from the shackles of colonialism continues to find expression in another prophetic statement: "If you strike a match in Africa, all of Europe will burn," said Haile Selassie in a 1936 speech to the League of Nations following Mussolini's invasion of Ethiopia.

Being French, Nostradamus had most to say about France in his writings, and if he neglects to name a country or place, we can safely assume he's talking about his native land. He means Paris, for example, when he says "the city" or simply "inside."

Obsessed by the Second World War overthrow of his nation's capital, he speaks in Century 4.80 of the failure of the "impregnable" Maginot Line, even remarking on its division into fifteen hydrographic sections:

> Near the great river, retrenchment, earth dug out,
> Into fifteen parts it will be divided by water,
> The city will be taken, fire, blood, cries, all turmoil,
> And most people confused by the shock.

Nostradamus foresaw Britain reacting strongly to German warmongering when he said:

> Those in the Isles long besieged
> Will take vigorous action against their enemies.
>
> (3.71)

He foretold how Hitler's plans to starve Britain during the war would fail, writing of the ferrying of supplies across the Atlantic before the periscopes of Nazi submarines:

> Where he thought to breed famine
> There will come plenty,
> While the eye of the sea watches like a greedy dog;
> For one to the other will give oil, wheat.
>
> (4.15)

There is another distinct reference to submarines — "when the fleet can swim under water" (3.13) — while Nostradamus forecasts different forms of modern transportation when he writes in 1.63: "People will travel safely through the sky, land, sea and wave." "Sea and wave" is not redundant, as ships pass through the waves and submarines through the sea.

Air warfare is a favorite theme with Nostradamus. With supreme nonchalance, he mentions airplanes and other technological wonders undreamt of in his day. "There will be wars for control of the clouds," he says baldly in Century 5.85, and "The armies will fight in the sky for a long time" (3.11). There's a graphic description of a twentieth century air battle, with searchlights, pilots wearing goggles and oxygen masks (making them look like strange beasts) and radio communications "heard" between the fighter planes:

Nostradamus called the U-boat periscopes "the eye of the sea," and also foretold of Germany's inability to stop Allied aid to Britain.

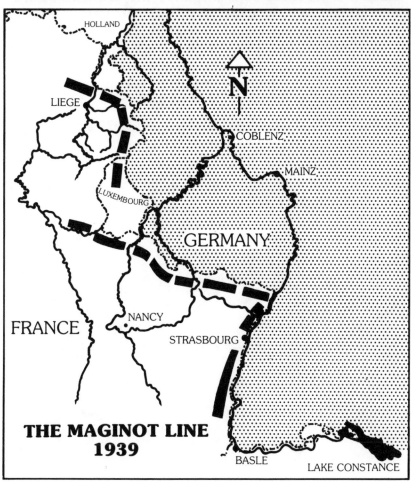

HOLLAND

LIEGE

LUXEMBOURG

COBLENZ

MAINZ

GERMANY

NANCY

FRANCE

STRASBOURG

**THE MAGINOT LINE
1939**

BASLE

LAKE CONSTANCE

The doomed Maginot Line, showing the fifteen hydrographic sections, each represented by a dash.

In 1842, long before the airplane was invented, English poet Alfred, Lord Tennyson predicted commercial air traffic and aerial warfare with its deadly droppings of "ghastly dew." In "Locksley Hall," he wrote:

Saw the heavens fill with
    commerce, argosies of
    magic sails,
Pilots of the purple
    twilight, dropping down
    with costly bales;
Heard the heavens fill with
    shouting, and there
    rained a ghastly dew
From the nations' airy
    navies grappling in the
    central blue.

They will think they have seen the sun at night,
When they see the pig half-man:
Noise, song, battle, fighting in the sky perceived:
And brute beasts will be heard to speak.

(1.64)

Nostradamus goes on to predict other marvels of science, including a manned space station circling 270 miles above the earth — the distance roughly equivalent to 100 leagues:

Samarobryn a hundred leagues from the hemisphere,
They will live without law, exempt from politics.

(6.5)

The origin of the name Samarobryn is, as yet, a mystery. But the quatrain is explicit in saying that whoever lives there will be free of the usual legal and political strictures. This is hard to accept, as space colonization will surely be carefully regulated if and when it happens. Or was Nostradamus contemplating a space station of extra-terrestrial invention?

A glimpse of the simple Montgolfier Balloon, more than two hundred years before its time, is given in Century 5.57:

There will go from Mont Gaulfier and Aventine
One who from the hole will warn the army.

A Maginot Line gun. Nostradamus saw what the French generals didn't: that the Line would not hold.

In 1794, the balloon was used for scouting at the Battle of Fleurus. The quatrain goes on to mention Pope Pius the Sixth, a contemporary of Montgolfier.

Nostradamus' vision swept across future time as well as homing in on specific events. He accurately forecast the rise, duration and fall of the British Empire, though he lived at a time before England had achieved supremacy on the seas:

> The great empire shall be held by England,
> The all-powerful for more than 300 years;
> Great forces will pass by land and sea,
> The Portuguese will not be pleased.

(10.100)

The British Empire began to grow around 1583. The Portuguese, with rich colonies and a powerful navy of their own, resented the empire building of another European nation. In further quatrains about England, Nostradamus writes with typical casualness of other developments. He mentions America, a nation that didn't exist in his day, and looking beyond our own time, he speaks of a "chief of London from the government of America," an intriguing Anglo-American connection.

So far-fetched, so improbable, so woebegone were many of Nostradamus' prophecies that it's easy to understand the way he felt when he wrote, "I was willing to be silent and to pass over what might be harmful, not only as relates to the present time, but also for the greater part of future time, since kingdoms, sects and religions will pass through stages so contrary, and indeed diametrically opposite, to their present state — that if I were to relate what will happen in the future, governors, sectaries and ecclesiastics would find it so little in accord with their auricular fancy that they would immediately condemn what future centuries will know and perceive to be true." This indeed seems to be the prophet's lot: to risk scorn and even persecution in predicting the downfall of those currently in power.

Nostradamus was brilliantly accurate in his predictions, even though some quatrains are so obliquely worded they could mean virtually anything. Many interpreters have been seduced by his linguistic mix of old French, Provencal, Latin, Greek and Italian sprinkled with anagrams and unknown names of people and places, and they've speculated wildly, using Nostradamus' texts to give wings to their own imaginings. It's not surprising that Nostradamus, one of very

The prophetess who delivered the divine responses to questions put to the ancient Greek oracle at Delphi was called the Pythia. For centuries, the Pythia was always a young virgin. Until, that is, a particularly attractive prophetess was seduced in the sacred cave; then the office was entrusted to elderly women. Young or old, the Pythia, who entered a trance-like state before uttering often inarticulate sounds that were interpreted by priests, was not expected to be knowledgeable or intelligent. But she had to be celibate.

few authors to have his works consistently in print for more than 400 years, has suffered the scorn of countless critics and detractors. The parade of scoffers began in 1558 with Laurens Videl's treatise entitled *Declaration of the Abuse, Ignorance and Sedition of Michel Nostradamus.* "Where do you get that stuff?" he snapped. "You intolerable pest, leading people astray with your false teachings full of abomination." And Eugene F. Parker, in an unpublished Harvard University doctoral thesis, wrote in 1920 that Nostradamus was inspired by a "profound scorn for the intelligence of his fellow men." Parker saluted our prophet this way: "All honor, then, to this king of pretenders who has been able to make his bluff good for over three and a half centuries. And the end of his reign is as yet far in the future."

Trial by Fire

Nostradamus made it clear his predictions extend to the year 3797, and forecast that a surfeit of horror and destruction will have to be endured before the earth is pacified "for a long time." The prophet could be speaking of our own time when he writes:

> After great trouble for humanity, a greater makes ready,
> The Great Mover renews the centuries:
> Rain, blood, milk, famine, steel and plague,
> In the heavens fire seen, a long spark running.
>
> (2.46)

The "long spark running" could be the projected reappearance, in February, 1986, of Halley's Comet — last seen in 1910 — that Nostradamus ties in with the outbreak of nuclear war:

> . . . . there will come
> Of people and beasts a dreadful destruction,
> Suddenly vengeance will be seen
> Hundred, hand, thirst, hunger, when the comet shall run.
>
> (2.62)

Nostradamus says the bringer of war will come out of the East, leading his rapacious armies across Europe and into France:

> The Oriental will leave his seat,
> He will pass the Apennine Mountains to see France:
> He will pierce the sky, the waters and the snow,
> And everyone will be struck with his rod.
>
> (2.29)

The warring leader is called the "third Antichrist" — number three in the breed of human beast that gave us Napoleon, then Hitler:

> The third Antichrist, soon annihilated,
> His bloody war will last twenty-seven years:
> Heretics will be slain, prisoners exiled,
> Blood, human bodies, reddened water and hail covering the
> earth.
>
> (8.77)

Paris will be razed by futuristic weapons "within the globes":

> There shall be unleashed live fire and hidden death
> Within the globes. Horrible! Frightful!
> By night the fleet will reduce the city to dust,
> The city on fire, the enemy indulgent.
>
> (5.8)

New York, "the new city," will be bombarded by missiles that will "burn" the sky at forty-five degrees. New York is situated between the fortieth and forty-fifth parallels:

> At forty-five degrees the sky will burn,
> Fire approaches the great new city,
> Instantly a great, scattered flame shall leap up.
>
> (6.97)

A resort area close to New York, referred to as "the garden of the world," will be bowled over by a tidal wave and its drinking supply poisoned. Note the reference to "hollow mountains," the prophet's old-fashioned way of describing skyscrapers:

> Garden of the world near the new city,
> In the path of the hollow mountains,
> It will be seized and plunged in the tank,
> They will be forced to drink waters poisoned by sulphur.
>
> (10.49)

What's more, on some future May 10 there will be a terrible earthquake — the sun in the 20th of Taurus points to that day:

> The sun in the 20th of Taurus the earth will tremble mightily,
> It will ruin the great theatre filled:
> The air, sky and land will be so dark and troubled
> That even unbelievers will call upon God and his saints.
>
> (9.83)

Ascletarion was a reckless prophet. He went so far as to predict the premature end of Roman Emperor Domitian (who ruled from 81 to 96 A.D.). Domitian, who had a perverse sense of humor, reciprocated by condemning him to death and demanded that Ascletarion predict just how he would be killed. "My body will be torn to pieces by dogs," was the seer's reply.

This was where Domitian, believing he could prove the futility of prophecy, hit upon a scheme. He carefully instructed his men to execute Ascletarion, burn his body and scatter the ashes in the River Tiber.

With the execution accomplished and the fortune-teller's body burning in accordance with the Emperor's wishes, a sudden Roman downpour doused the flames and sent the executioners running for shelter. It was then that a pack of dogs pounced on the half-burnt corpse and tore it to pieces.

Century 10.67 repeats the prediction of disaster:

A very mighty trembling in the month of May,
. . . . Hail will fall larger than an egg.

Modern experts in the politics of food have warned against losing the battle against hunger, a danger Nostradamus already saw:

The great famine that I see approaching,
Often turning, then becoming universal.
It will be so vast and long that they will pull
Roots from the trees and babes from the breast.

(1.67)

And so Nostradamus piles one calamity on top of another. He shares one prediction with many other seers, great and small: the horror of horrors will coincide with the turn of the century. In Century 1.16 he writes:

Plague, famine, death by the military hand,
The century approaches renewal.

He even names the month and year in Century 10.72:

In the year 1999 and seven months,
From the skies shall come a great king of terror,
To bring back to life the great king of the Mongols,
Before and after, Mars reigns happily.

This age, which many of us will live to see, will be so deeply plunged into strife that we will despair of ever seeing its resolution. Yet Nostradamus is comforting in the end: there *is* reason for hope:

Mars and the sceptre will be in conjunction,
Under Cancer, a calamitous war:
A little while after there will be a new king anointed
Who for a long time shall pacify the earth.

(6.24)

The sceptre stands for Jupiter and, according to Dr. Christian Wollner who published *The Mystery of Nostradamus* in 1926, this conjunction with Mars under Cancer can only occur on June 21, 2002. Peace finally gains a foothold:

At last the wolf, the lion, ox and ass,
The timid deer, shall lie down with the mastiffs.

(10.99)

Having left us with this final vision of harmony, Nostradamus died in Salon in 1566 and was buried in the vault at the Church of St. Lawrence. His epitaph, translated from the original Latin, reads:

> Here rest the bones of the illustrious Michel Nostradamus, alone of all mortals judged worthy to record with his almost divine pen, under the influence of the stars, the future events of the entire world. He lived sixty-two years, six months and seventeen days.

So far, we've had to rely on the passing of time to successfully interpret Nostradamus' work. While confessing that he "sought to polish" his predictions "a bit obscurely" and admitting that most of his verses were "so ticklish there is no making way through them," he believed that someday the foggy quatrains would become clear. "For although they are written under a cloud," Nostradamus averred, "the meanings will be understood."

Glencoe in the Scottish
Highlands where seclusion
and solitary steadfastness of
purpose inspired the strange
faculty of Second Sight.

4 Highland Second Sight

"The second sight is an impression made either by the mind upon the eye or the eye upon the mind, by which things distant or future are perceived and seen as if they were present."

Dr. Samuel Johnson

Long, long ago, the earliest settlers of the rugged Scottish Highlands told the future in the strangest of ways. "Consulting the fates," they called it. They would examine stones for hours on end, wait all night at the tombs of brave men and endure lonely vigils in the fields wrapped in cow hides. One cruel rite consisted of roasting a live cat on a spit and waiting for its screams to draw other cats whose order and manner of appearance would deliver a prophetic message. A late Stone Age priesthood practiced a ritual of contacting the spirits of dead ancestors they believed inhabited their stone circles and burial mounds. Those priests able to foretell the future were thought to have been granted their powers by spirits who later came to be known as fairies.

From these barbaric beginnings, there developed among the people of the mountains and moorland the gift — or curse — of second sight in which certain Highlanders, usually against their will, were possessed by visions of the future. Seeing these visions could be uncomfortable or even traumatic. According to Martin Martin who wrote *Description of the Western Isles* in 1705, "the eyelids of the person are erected and the eyes continue staring until the object vanishes." He mentions a luckless seer on the Isle of Skye "whose eyelids turned up so far inwards that he had to draw them down with his fingers or get others to do so."

The Brahan Seer

The most revered of all the Highland prophets is Coinneach Odhar, or the Brahan Seer. One after another, his predictions have come true. And though he's been dead more than 300 years, several of his forecasts — including a prediction of the utter desolation of Scotland by "horrid black rains" — are still pending. Born on the Island of Lewis in the Outer Hebrides, he moved to the mainland in the mid-seventeenth century to work as a turf-cutter on Lord Seaforth's estate near Inverness. The prophet, who was one-eyed, always carried a smooth pebble with a hole in it to "see" the events he foretold. His short-range pronouncements were so uncannily accurate that his reputation quickly spread throughout the High-

Lady Seaforth — her fury led to the Brahan Seer being thrust head-first into a barrel of boiling tar.

lands. We know little about Coinneach's personal life, but we do know he had a sharp wit that belied his humble occupation. It was his sometimes malicious straightforwardness — combined with his under-estimation of Lady Seaforth's vengeful nature — that earned him the cruelest of deaths.

He got into trouble while Lord Seaforth was away in Paris on business. Lady Seaforth, anxious about her husband's extended absence, called Coinneach from the fields. In front of her principal retainers, she asked him whether her Lord was safe and what he was doing. The Brahan Seer responded by raising the divination stone to his blind eye and laughing out loud. "Fear not for your Lord," he said at last. "He is safe and sound, well and hearty, merry and happy." Naturally, Lady Seaforth pressed Coinneach for more details, which he was loath to give. But the seer's silence was scornful, and Lady Seaforth demanded to be told the whole story. Secretly reveling, we suspect, in his disclosures, Coinneach made a show of reluctance before revealing that he saw Lord Seaforth "in a gay-gilded room, grandly decked out in velvets, with silks and cloth of gold, and on his knees before a fair lady, his arm round her waist, and her hand pressed to his lips." Lady Seaforth burned with jealousy and anger. But rather than condemn her husband, she accused the Brahan Seer of slandering the Lord's name and immediately sentenced him to death for "defaming a mighty chief in the midst of his vassals."

The Brahan Seer waited for her fury to subside. When he finally realized she would not recant, he drew out his stone, pressed it to his unseeing eye and pronounced what has come to be called the Doom of the Seaforths:

> I see into the far future, and I read the doom of the race of my oppressor. The long descended line of Seaforth will, ere many generations have passed, end in extinction and sorrow. I see a chief, the last of his house, both deaf and dumb. He will be the father of four fair sons, all of whom he will follow to the tomb. . . After lamenting over the last and most promising of his sons, he himself shall sink into the grave, and the remnant of his possessions shall be inherited by a white-coifed lassie from the East, and she is to kill her sister. And as a sign by which it may be known that these things are coming to pass, there shall be four great lairds in the days of the last deaf and dumb Seaforth — Gairloch, Chisholm, Grant and Raasay —

Thomas the Rhymer, a thirteenth century Scottish seer, was one of the very few secular prophets to receive the wholehearted blessing of the Church. Archbishop John Spottiswood (1565-1639) wrote in *History of the Church of Scotland* that Rhymer "may be justly admired, having foretold to many ages before, the Union of England and Scotland in the ninth degree of Bruce's blood, with the succession of Bruce himself to the crown, being yet a child, and other divers particulars which the event hath satisfied and made good."

Witches told Macbeth, the Scottish tyrant immortalized by Shakespeare, that he wouldn't suffer defeat "until Birnam wood do come to Dunsinane." Since Dunsinane was his castle, Macbeth understood this prediction to mean he would never be vanquished. But in 1054 Birnam wood did indeed appear to be advancing on the castle: the soldiers of Siward, earl of Northumbria, carried hundreds of lopped off branches from the forest to camouflage their attack. Siward's men won the ensuing battle and the witches' prophecy was fulfilled.

of whom one shall be buck-toothed, another hare-lipped, another half-witted, and the fourth a stammerer.

This tirade incensed Lady Seaforth further and the seer was seized, bound hand and foot and marched off to Chanonry Point (where, in 1969, a town council memorial stone was erected in his honor) to be thrust head-first into a barrel of boiling tar. To make his death even more agonizing, the inside of the barrel had been sewn thickly with long, sharp spikes driven in from the outside.

The Brahan Seer suffered the fate of those predictors who dared prophesy the reversal of the *status quo*. If there's a heaven and if he reached it, he must have watched with satisfaction as the house of Seaforth withered and died according to his prediction. Few forecasts can match this one; every detail has come true. The history books tell us that the last Lord Seaforth was deaf and dumb, that none of his four sons survived his death in 1815, that each of the four lairds named as contemporaries of the last Seaforth was either buck-toothed, hare-lipped, half-witted or afflicted with stammering. Further, we know that the "white-coifed lassie from the East," in the form of Lord Seaforth's eldest surviving daughter, inherited the property after returning from India. She did inadvertently kill her younger sister, Caroline, in 1823 while at the reins of a runaway pony carriage that threw them both to the ground. Much of the Seaforth estate was later sold, completing Coinneach's vengeful prediction.

Robert Bain tells in his *History of Ross* (1899) how Coinneach also forecast the decline of the once-proud Fairburn family:

During the middle of the 17th Century no branch of the House of Kintail possessed more apparent vitality than the Fairburn Family. But the seer, guided by his mysterious prescience, saw that their decay was imminent, and that the worm was about to eat them like wool. A time was at hand, he said, when they would disappear from the land, and when their Tower would so become a desolation that a cow would bring forth a calf in its topmost room. The latter event occurred precisely as stated in the present century. The Tower had become a ruin and a receptacle for straw, and the historic cow, the property of a distant relative of the present writer, attracted by the fodder scattered about, ascended the spiral stair, and while there gave birth to the calf. By no persuasion, however, could she be brought to descend by the way she came, and had to be lowered by ropes to the ground.

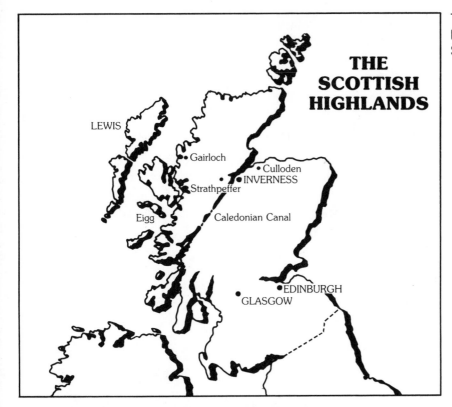

THE
SCOTTISH
HIGHLANDS

LEWIS

• Gairloch

• Culloden
• INVERNESS

Strathpeffer

Eigg

Caledonian Canal

• EDINBURGH
GLASGOW

The Scottish Highlands: the home territory of Second Sight.

More than eighty years before the Battle of Culloden Moor, the Brahan Seer walked across the field near Inverness, and noticing an old mill, remarked:

> The day will come when thy wheel shall be turned for three successive days with water red with human blood; for on thy lade's bank a fierce battle shall be fought in which much blood will be spilt.

On another visit to the area, this first impression was confirmed; once more, he felt the horror of the coming slaughter:

> . . . thy bleak moor shall, ere many generations have passed away, be stained with the best blood of the Highlands. Glad am I that I will not see that day, for it will be a fearful period; heads will be lopped off by the score, and no mercy will be shown or quarter given on either side.

In 1746, most of the six thousand Highlanders who faced the English Redcoats at Culloden were massacred in less than an hour in the last battle to be fought on British soil.

One hundred and fifty years before the building of the Caledonian Canal, an Inverness businessman sent for Coinneach. With his note-book in his hand, the man asked for a recital of the seer's prophecies. But when he heard,

> Strange as it may seem to you this day, the time will come, and it is not far off, when full-rigged ships will be seen sailing eastward and westward by the back of Tomnahurich,

he flung the notes into the fire and ordered him from his office. Yet in 1822, the Caledonian Canal was completed and ships sailed around the back of Tomnahurich Hill behind the city. The Brahan Seer foresaw other marvels of the coming Industrial Revolution — gas and water pipes, for example:

The cottage around which raged the Battle of Culloden Moor. Coinneach Odhar predicted the battle more than eighty years before "the best blood of the Highlands" was spilled.

> . . . fire and water shall run in streams through all the streets and lanes of Inverness.

And the railway:

> . . . long strings of carriages without horses shall run between Dingwall and Inverness.

Although its pumprooms are now closed, the Highland town of Strathpeffer is still celebrated for its mineral waters. The community enjoyed its greatest popularity after people heard about a letter written in 1818 by Dr. Thomas Morrison of Elsick, Aberdeenshire to the administrators of Ross County in which he expressed his thanks for "health restored from an illness which for fifteen years had baffled the leading medical practitioners in Britain." The Brahan

The Caledonian Canal. Its construction gave a posthumous boost to the Brahan Seer's reputation.

Perhaps the most famous prediction in history is the warning to Julius Caesar: "Beware the Ides of March."

On the way to the Forum on March 15, 44 B.C., Caesar met Vestricius Spurinna, the seer who "saw" the danger to the Roman emperor while examining the entrails of a sacrificial animal. "Well, Spurinna," he said, "the Ides of March are come." "Aye, Caesar," replied Spurinna. "Come but not gone." An hour later Caesar was dead — the victim of twenty-three dagger thrusts.

Seer, musing in the days when Strathpeffer's wells were less appreciated, predicted the spa's boom with these words:

> Uninviting and disagreeable as it now is, with its thick crusted surface and unpleasant smell, the day will come when it shall be under lock and key, and crowds of pleasure and health seekers shall be seen thronging its portals, in their eagerness to get a draught of its waters.

The people of Inverness are convinced Coinneach Odhar predicted the Second World War; after all, he forecast a frightful disaster would strike the world when it was possible to cross the River Ness dryshod in five places. In the last days of August, 1939, a temporary bridge was opened to relieve the strain on the city's old condemned suspension bridge. That made five spans across the river. On September 1, 1939, Hitler's troops marched into Poland.

Of Coinneach's several forecasts yet to be realized, the most feared is this one:

> The day will come when the jaw-bone of the big sheep will put the plough on the rafters; when sheep shall become so numerous that the bleating of the one shall be heard by the other from Conchra in Lochalsh to Bun-da-Loch in Kintail, they shall be at their height in price, and henceforth will go back and deteriorate, until they disappear altogether, and be so thoroughly forgotten that a man finding the jaw-bone of a sheep in a cairn, will not recognize it, or be able to tell what animal it belonged to. The ancient proprietors of the soil shall give place to strange merchant proprietors, and the whole Highlands will become one huge deer forest; the whole country will be so utterly desolated and depopulated that the crow of a cock shall not be heard north of Druim-Uachdair; the people will emigrate to islands now unknown, but which shall yet be discovered in the boundless oceans after which the deer and other wild animals in the huge wilderness shall be exterminated and browned by horrid black rains. The people will then return and take undisturbed possession of the lands of their ancestors.

In that it traces the rise and fall of sheep farming in northern Scotland, part of the prophecy is already fulfilled. And it's true that vast stretches of the Highlands are owned by absentee landlords who've stocked the land with game, while "merchant proprietors" have proliferated in the wake of recent offshore oil finds. The ques-

The monument of a kilted highlander at Glenfinnan, Inverness, the place Bonnie Prince Charlie unfurled his father's standard on August 19, 1745.

tion that remains is what the Brahan Seer meant by "horrid black rains?" Was he talking about nuclear fall-out, or had he anticipated a giant, oil-related explosion? Time, as always, will tell.

The Passing of Vision

Highland writings spanning the 300 years up to the beginning of this century are rife with accounts of second sight. Among the most bizarre comes from Lord Tarbut, who served as a member of King Charles II's Privy Council. In a letter, he described how the seers of the Isle of Harris saw an arrow in the thigh of a certain islander, although the man died without such a wound. But that was only the beginning of the story. It so happened that while carrying the man's corpse to the churchyard on an open bier, the pallbearers were rankled by the approach of a second cortege. An argument broke out between the two groups as to whose funeral should be held first. A fight started, and one of the more aggressive mourners, who was armed, let fly with an arrow. He fulfilled the prediction to perfection: the arrow lodged in the dead man's thigh!

The year 1707 saw the publication of a little book of second sightings collected by Reverend John Frazer of Tiree. Eye-witness accounts tumble out one after another, each more compelling than the last. There's a story of a servant who slept nightly in a barn until

Henry IV of England (who reigned from 1399 to 1413) had a great respect for the predictors of his age. So great, in fact, that when he was told he would die in Jerusalem, he called off a planned journey to the Holy Land. He might as well have made the trip. For his death happened unexpectedly at Westminster Abbey — in the Jerusalem Chamber!

he saw a vision of a corpse lying in the hay. Six months later, one of his fellow workers fell ill and died. The night before the funeral, the dead man's family brought the corpse to the barn and laid it in the same spot foreseen by the visionary servant.

Then there's the eerie tale of the seer on the tiny Isle of Eigg. Beginning in 1685, he repeatedly warned the people to flee for their lives. For, said he, the island would be invaded by "a people of strange and different habits and arms" who would kill, rape, burn and plunder. A few people took him seriously and left for the mainland, but most dismissed his words. In June, 1689, the seer fell sick and some of the islanders hastened to his bedside to ask him to take back his prediction. He replied by telling them to be patient, for they would soon witness the truth of his warning. And so he died, a prophet without honor on his own island. Without honor, that is, until two weeks later. Without any hint of their coming save the admonitions of the dead seer, a band of heavily-armed English Redcoats landed to overrun the little community.

In 1763, a treatise by Theophilus Insulanus — believed to be plain old Mr. Macpherson, a minister on the Isle of Skye — was published in Edinburgh, chronicling a host of Highland prophecies and visions. They included the story of a young girl who had envisioned a corpse draped with black cloth being carried up through a pass by half a dozen men. Twelve years later, a corpse was borne up a nearby cliff in the way the girl described after a local woman had fallen to her death while gathering herbs. There was the case of another woman who, as she sat by her fireside, "saw" a local man take one of her sheep and cut its throat. She immediately went to the man's house, forced open the door and caught him in that very act. The thief offered her several lengths of linen in recompense and pleaded with her not to reveal his crime to the neighbors!

Dr. Samuel Johnson stated in *A Journey to the Western Isles of Scotland* that he and his biographer James Boswell found it most difficult to communicate with the Highland seers during their trip in 1773. "There is one living in Skye, with whom we would have gladly conversed; but he was very gross and ignorant, and knew no English," he wrote. What a shame Dr. Johnson didn't meet Reverend John Morrison, a minister in Petty, near Inverness, who presented his second sight with an eloquence and humor Johnson would have appreciated. Known as the Petty Seer, Morrison made his most famous of prophetic utterances in church when he exclaimed:

Ye sinful and stiff-necked people, God will, unless ye turn from your evil ways, sweep you ere along into a place of torment. And as a sign of what I say, *Clach dubh an Abain*, large though it be, will be carried soon, without human agency, a considerable distance seawards.

Clach dubh an Abain is a massive stone weighing at least eight tons, located at the time on the south shore of the Bay of Petty. Morrison's congregation had to wait a long time for the fulfillment of this prophecy but fulfillment there was some twenty-six years later. On February 20, 1799, the stone was somehow carried 260 yards out into the bay where it can still be seen today.

Another Morrison vignette describes him stepping out of his manse with his violin to gently chastize a group of drunken fisherwomen returning from market. Shamed though the women were at being tipsy in the minister's company, one of them was bold enough to

The northwest coast of Scotland: the haunt of long-gone seers.

Michael Scot, astrologer and confidant of Frederick II (1194-1250) predicted his death would be caused by an object falling on his head. Accordingly, he was always on the alert when he left a building and was most careful to avoid any dangerous structures. But the falling object got him anyway. While at prayer in a cathedral a loose stone plummeted from the roof onto his head, killing him instantly.

ask him for a tune. He complied, and soon the unsteady assembly was dancing in the street. Later, one of the church elders heard of the minister's conduct and headed for his house to reprimand him. Morrison replied, "How could I refuse to play a tune for one for whom the holy angels themselves will soon be tuning their harps?" Within a week, the woman became ill and died.

As time wore on, the instances of second sight were restricted to images of skulls, corpses, ghosts and funerals. It was as if the visions themselves were mourning the inroads being made into the Highlands' isolation. Gone were the grand, sweeping prophecies of yesteryear. Though death had always made regular appearances, the gifted ones now could see nothing else. An Inverness-shire crofter, who seldom failed to "see" a phantom funeral before the actual event, was typical of those who experienced second sight in the late nineteenth century. Fearing he might have bad news to impart, the man's neighbors did all they could to keep out of his way. And the crofter, only too aware that he'd become the local outcast, vowed to keep his visions to himself. Not that it made his own life any easier. He kept seeing phantom funerals.

Sometimes he *felt* them, too. One day as he was about to cross a bridge near his home, he stepped aside to let another ghostly funeral procession go by. As it passed, one of the phantom horses reared up and kicked him in the leg. The blow was unmistakable. Pain shot through his leg and he was forced to limp home where, in spite of his complaint, his family could find no proof of the injury. Next day, the crofter was about to cross the same bridge when he met a real funeral — the material version of the previous day's vision. Sure enough, the same horse lashed out and kicked him in exactly the same spot as before. Once more he limped home, this time with a bruise to back up his story. But he told his family the kick from the phantom horse was just as painful as the one delivered by its more substantial version!

Since the turn of the century, even the incidence of death visions has declined dramatically. Highland second sight, once "a fact indisputable in almost every one of the more rural communities," according to a Scottish authority named Logan, has dwindled to a few isolated occurences. It seems seclusion and solitary steadfastness of purpose are required for the faculty to flourish. Without doubt, the decline is connected with the encroachment of the motor car and the telephone. Perhaps the gift was ingrained in home ground as, even in the old days, second sight was lost once seers were removed from their hardy environment. Lord Tarbut, writing toward the end of the seventeenth century, told how Highland prophets never again experienced visions "when transported to live in other countries, especially in America . . ."

Not that the seers were complaining. As diarist John Aubrey mentions in his *Miscellanies* (1696), second sight "is a thing very troublesome to them that have it." For the rest of us, however, the fading of these visions represents another regrettable victory of the ordinary over the extraordinary, another whittling of our sense of wonder. Another shroud over the Unknown.

II THE CRYSTAL BALL AND THE CROSS

The ancient links between spirituality and prediction have continued right through to the present day. Edgar Cayce, the prophet of geological upheaval, was a kindly, humble man who read his Bible daily. The ubiquitous Jeane Dixon may have sold herself to talk shows and TV commercials, but her life is rooted in Christian devotion. And the ranks of the most celebrated of modern psychics include a Baptist minister and a Christian Spiritualist. Not that psychic intuition favors the religiously inclined only. Neither faith nor belief, but rather the extraordinary ability to resonate with otherworldly vibrations singles out the psychic . . .

Edgar Cayce: selfless, God-fearing and still ''America's most mysterious man.''

5 Edgar Cayce

"What happens to us
Is irrelevant to the world's geology
But what happens to the world's geology
Is not irrelevant to us."

Hugh MacDiarmid

The Gentle Seer

Edgar Cayce was an unlikely mystic and a reluctant prophet. The mild-mannered family man who studied his Bible daily and accepted reincarnation as a fact of life certainly didn't *look* like "America's Most Mysterious Man." And Cayce, we can't help but think, didn't *feel* much like a prophetic figure either. Untouched by the fuss that accompanied his pronouncements, he saw himself as less of a predictor, more as someone privileged to help and guide the ordinary people who waited anxiously to hear the voice of Universal Consciousness speak through him.

Cayce was gaunt and balding with a receding chin and eyes that twinkled behind rimless glasses — hardly anyone's picture of a prophet. Yet his method was mystical enough: he would "sleep" in order to predict. First, he would take off his jacket and tie and loosen his collar and shoelaces. Then he would lie on the couch in his study, fold his arms across his chest, close his eyes and breathe deeply as his wife or secretary guided him into a state of self-hypnosis. Cayce would then answer the inquiries of the sick, needy, fearful and distraught in a series of often cryptically worded sentences. Mostly he gave spiritual advice, trying to find a way around obstacles in careers and relationships. But he also pointed to the whereabouts of oil wells and buried treasure and gave tips to businessmen worried about the location of their holdings or the stability of their stocks and bonds. As Cayce's fame grew, so did the pressure for answers and remedies. In the end, the clamoring of a vampire public — and Cayce's willingness to serve as many souls as possible — sucked the very lifeblood from him.

A map of the "many physical changes of a minor or greater degree" that Edgar Cayce foresaw.

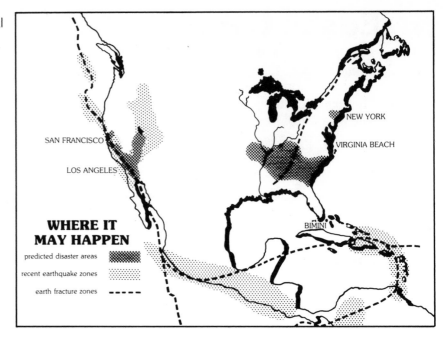

WHERE IT
MAY HAPPEN

predicted disaster areas

recent earthquake zones

earth fracture zones

NEW YORK

VIRGINIA BEACH

SAN FRANCISCO

LOS ANGELES

BIMINI

The Earth Changes its Face

The slumbering prophet predicted the First and Second World Wars, the independence of India and the 1929 stock market crash. He also hit upon the year that saw the end of the last war and foretold — fifteen years before the event — the creation of the State of Israel. The world awaits fulfillment of the most catastrophic of all the Cayce prophecies: a devastating succession of earthquakes that will rupture continents and transform the global map.

Cayce forecast the destruction by the end of this century of New York, Los Angeles and San Francisco. He said that "the greater portion of Japan must go into the sea" and that northern Europe "will be changed as in the twinkling of an eye." He went on: "Even many of the battlefields of the present [he was speaking in 1941] will be ocean, will be the seas, the bays, the lands over which the new order will carry on their trade as one with another." Across North America he saw "many physical changes of a minor or greater degree" with "the greater change" being in the North Atlantic seabord. As early as 1934, Cayce said:

> The earth will be broken up in many places. The early portion will see a change in the physical aspect of the west coast of America. There will appear open waters in the northern portions

of Greenland. There will be seen new lands of the Caribbean Sea. . . South America will be shaken from the uppermost portion to the end; and in the Antarctic off Tierra del Fuego will be land, and a strait with rushing waters.

Cayce later offered more detail on the American upheavals:

Watch New York, Connecticut and the like. Many portions of the East coast will be disturbed, as well as many portions of the West coast, as well as the central portion of the United States.

Los Angeles, San Francisco, most all of these will be among those that will be destroyed before New York, even.

Portions of the now East coast of New York, or New York City itself, will in the main disappear. This will be another generation, though, here; while the southern portions of Carolina, Georgia, these will disappear. This will be much sooner.

The waters of the Great Lakes will empty into the Gulf of Mexico.

If there are greater activities in Vesuvius or Pelée, then the southern coast of California — and the areas between Salt Lake and the southern portions of Nevada — may expect, within three months following same, an inundation caused by the earthquakes.

Mounting tension over a rash of earthquake predictions in San Francisco was eased by Mayor John Alioto's defiant announcement of a grand Earthquake Party in the city's Civic Center Plaza. To mark the sixty-third anniversary of the Great Quake of 1906, the party was held at 5:13 a.m. on April 18, 1969. Yawning celebrants rolled up in the thousands.

Cayce's prophecies of geological upheaval cover 1936 to 1998, from the initial tilting of the earth's axis to the destruction of New York. He anticipated that the axis would be shifted by the year 2001, bringing on reversals in climate: ". . . where there have been those [areas] of a frigid or semi-tropical [nature] will become the more tropical, and moss and fern will grow . . ." We will know the earth changes have come "when there is the first breaking up of some conditions in the South Sea [the South Pacific] and those as apparent in the sinking or rising of that which is almost opposite it, or in the Mediterranean, and the Aetna [Etna] area. Then we may know it has begun."

A marked increase in volcanic and earthquake activity since the sixties has already jolted skeptics who laughed at the suggestion of geological disturbances. As if in answer to Cayce's warning, restless Mount Etna erupted with greater than usual violence in 1964 and 1971, and on August 4, 1979, the volcano unleashed its awesome power in the most spectacular eruption in decades. Villagers in nearby Fornazzo evacuated their homes and Sicily's eastern coastal city of Catania was showered with ash, cinders and rocks for the first time in twenty years. The fiery explosions could be seen from the Italian mainland forty-six miles to the northeast. The 1964 earthquake in Alaska — the strongest ever recorded on the North American continent — pushed seismic waves all the way to Antarctica. An earthquake in China killed more than 655,000 people in 1976 and, that same year, more than 22,000 died in a quake in Guatemala. The 1970s have seen major earthquakes all across the world, from Peru to Pakistan, from Yugoslavia to the Philippines. In April, 1979, thousands were evacuated from the Caribbean isle of St. Vincent to escape the eruptions of Mount Soufrière. Within

A lava fountain in Honolulu. "We want to know if it will happen where we are," wrote Cayce. "What difference does it make, if we are living right?"

a few days, tremors were felt along the New England coast, one of Cayce's "danger zones." Meanwhile, the 600 mile San Andreas fault that runs down the California coast is being nervously watched. As recently as August 6, 1979, northern California's coastal fault zone was hit by the strongest quake in sixty-eight years. Then on October 15, 1979, more tremors rumbled through Imperial Valley, leaving scores of people injured and causing $10 million worth of property damage.

Cayce pointed to his adopted home of Virginia Beach and nearby Norfolk as "safety lands." Other safe areas cited were "parts of Ohio, Indiana and Illinois and much of the southern portion of Canada and the eastern portion of Canada." Yet safety was hardly

"Los Angeles, San Francisco, most all of these will be among those that will be destroyed . . . " Cayce predicted.

By Jove, there's trouble brewing in space!

According to scientists John Gribbin and Stephen Plagemann, authors of *The Jupiter Effect* (1974), the earth will be racked with earthquakes sometime in 1982 when all the planets in our solar system align themselves on the same side of the sun. The cumulative pull of their gravities will disturb solar equilibrium and cause the sun to tug at the earth's crust. Jupiter (Jove, to the Romans), the largest planet, will be the most disruptive influence.

Gribbin and Plagemann confine their earthquake predictions to California. They warn that "hundreds of thousands" of people could be killed when the planets — which repeat this dangerous alignment every 179 years — combine to upset the already unstable San Andreas fault.

Cayce's preoccupation. While understanding his listeners' anxieties, he made his dire geological predictions with the air of a man utterly resigned to Fate. "Right away," he wrote in February, 1933, "we want to know if it will happen where we are. What difference does it make, if we are living right?"

In 1931, in the throes of the Great Depression, Edgar Cayce made the observation that depressions came and went in cycles of twenty-four to twenty-five years. So it was that 1954 was termed a "recession" period. And again, 1978 was a poor year for the American economy, with the sagging dollar being symptomatic of the slump. Cayce also said there would be economic upheavals after World War Two which would cause "more and more upsetting in the monetary units of the land." To escape this strife, he counseled people to flee the city for the subsistence living of the country. Return to the land, he urged in his readings, ". . . because of hardships which have not yet begun in this country, so far as the supply and demand for foods is concerned." He said that anyone who can buy a farm is fortunate: "Buy it if you don't want to grow hungry in some days to come," he told a would-be farmer. And to a man who was pondering whether to sell his land, Cayce instructed, "Hold the acreage, for that may be the basis for the extreme periods through which all portions of the country must pass." Speaking of the food crisis that must come, he said: "Saskatchewan, the Pampas area of the Argentine . . . portions of South Africa . . . these rich areas, with some portions of Montana and Nevada, must feed the world."

Cayce's own ties with the soil were strong; he was born in 1877 on a farm near Hopkinsville, Kentucky. His gift of clairvoyance first appeared at the age of six when he was able to see and talk to "visions." When he was a little older, he discovered to his delight that he could sleep on his schoolbooks and absorb what was inside them. For a while, the sleeping scholar worked wonders in the classroom, but this skill soon failed him and "America's Most Mysterious Man," a title conferred on him posthumously by the comic book *House of Mystery*, became a sixth grade dropout. In time, his work was to be the subject of Ph.D. theses, but in his youth he labored wherever he could find work: on a farm, in a shoe store, in a bookstore, as a salesman and photographer.

Then, at twenty-one years of age, came an event that launched his career. His throat muscles seized up slowly and mysteriously, and no doctor could find the cause. As a last resort, Cayce managed to re-enter the same kind of trance he had known as a boy. A strong, clear voice came to him and recommended medication and physical therapy that finally restored his muscular tissue.

From that moment on, Cayce's true vocation began. He entered these trances, or "sleeps," to diagnose illnesses and prescribe treatments. It made no difference whether the people he examined were in the same room or hundreds of miles away. Local doctors took advantage of his skills to find out what ailed their patients and, on October 9, 1910, the *New York Times* galvanized public interest in Cayce by running a two-page article on the man and his work. He progressed from medical to psychic readings, and the more exact his words were, the more people lined up to have their lives touched by his unique powers.

Those who acted on Cayce's prediction about Virginia Beach are wealthy today, for he pointed to a boom in local real estate that materialized fifteen years after his death. Population figures alone demonstrate the sudden rapid growth of Virginia Beach. The surfside hamlet of 5,000 people in the early fifties had grown, by 1976, to a resort of 225,000. On August 27, 1932, Cayce spoke of a magnificent future for neighboring Norfolk: ". . . within the next thirty years — Norfolk, with its environs, is to be the chief port on the East coast, this is not excepting Philadelphia or New York . . ." Sure enough, in 1957 Norfolk became the eastern seaboard's largest port and its growth continued to outstrip its rivals. By 1964, Norfolk's annual cargo shipments had topped 60 million tons against 48 million for New York and 21 million for Philadelphia. Today, Norfolk handles more coal than any other port district in the world.

World Born Again

Ranking among Cayce's most sweeping and, at this point, unlikely predictions is his vision of a free Soviet Union being "born again." From Russia's religious development will stem "the greater hope of the world." Cayce foresaw an alliance with the United States helping Russia into this dramatic new position, speaking of the Soviet Union being "guided" by "that friendship with the nation that hath even set on its present monetary unit: 'In God We Trust.' " In China, too, Cayce saw an unprecedented stirring of Christianity:

> This here, will be one day the cradle of Christianity, as applied in the lives of men. Yea, it is far off as man counts time, but only a day in the heart of God. For tomorrow China will awake.

". . . we're likely to find more amazing things at the bottom of the sea than on all the surfaces of the rest of the planets." — Thor Heyerdahl, explorer, leader of the famed Kon Tiki expedition.

Peter the Great of Russia (1672-1725) seemed to know all about the future growth and domination of the Soviet Union. His last will and testament contained these words:

I found Russia a rivulet; I shall leave it a river; and my successors will make of it a great ocean, destined to fecundate Europe, and its waters will overflow the whole continent, in spite of the dykes with which weak hands seek to restrain it, if my descendants understand how to direct its course.

We might tend to view these prophecies as the desires of a God-fearing man rather than prediction in the usual sense. Yet considering the deeply religious character of the Russian people and the Christian stirrings in neighboring Poland during the Pope's spring, 1979 visit, Cayce may not be far from the truth.

While the United States is regarded worldwide as a nation more egalitarian than most, Cayce, seeing some citizens were more equal than others, spoke of "the leveling" to come. With these words, uttered in 1938, he foresaw the American race riots of the late 60s:

Though there may come those periods when there will be great stress, as brother rises against brother, as group or sect or race rises against race — yet the leveling must come.

Cayce also gave warning of a full-scale revolution in the United States, urging "those in position to give of their means, their wealth, their education, their position" to heed the gap between themselves and less privileged members of society:

For unless these are considered, there must eventually become a revolution in this country — and there will be a dividing of the sections as one against another. For these are the leveling means and manners to which men resort when there is the plenty in some areas and a lack of sustenance in the life of others.

An even more sinister prediction, recorded in 1940, warns of a time when much of the world is oppressed and conflict rages within the U.S.:

When many of the isles of the sea and many of the lands have come under the subjugation of those who fear neither man nor the devil; who rather join themselves with that force by which they may proclaim might and power as right, as of a superman who is to be an ideal for a generation to be established, then shall thy own land see the blood flow, as in those periods when brother fought against brother.

On June 28, 1940, Edgar Cayce spoke excitedly of the rising of parts of the lost continent of Atlantis, a fabled land that has captured the interest and imagination of more and more people in the last decade. "Expect it in '68 and '69," he declared. "Not so far away!" Cayce was referring to the area around the Bahamian isle of Bimini which he maintained is "the highest portion left above the waves of a once great continent." While Atlantis remains to be officially rediscovered, a fishing guide found a submerged pattern of symmetrically-shaped stones off Bimini in the summer of 1968. The find precipitated a rash of expeditions to the area, one of which uncovered chunks of marble pillars lodged near an underwater road.

Cayce was as able to perceive our unknown past as our unwritten future. He referred to Atlantis 700 times in his readings, placing the sunken land mass between the Gulf of Mexico and the Mediterranean. The readings maintain the lost continent, whose civilization was technologically superior to our own, was rent by a series of man-made and natural cataclysms between 15,600 and 10,000 B.C. It all started with the mishandling of a Great Crystal or Firestone used to focus solar energy. Explosions generated by the crystal brought on intense volcanic activity which finally plunged the torn remains of Atlantis beneath the ocean. Many Atlanteans, having learned of the impending disaster through the prophecies of their leaders, managed to flee to other parts of the world. "Evidence of Atlantean civilization," said Cayce, "may be found in the Pyrenees and Morocco and in British Honduras, Yucatan and parts of the Americas — especially near Bimini and in the Gulf Stream in this vicinity." He predicted that identical records would be found in Bimini, Egypt and on Mexico's Yucatan peninsula. "The records are one," he insisted.

Trouble in Detroit. Said Cayce: "Though there may come those periods when there will be great stress, as brother rises against brother . . . yet the leveling must come."

Meanwhile, reincarnated Atlanteans will be drawn to rebuild the emergent homeland:

> There are, as has been given, many peoples being born again into the earth's plane who were, through their experiences, in this land. With the building, then, again, we find the innate desire will come to an innumerable number to be in some manner or way associated — either as dwellers for a portion of the time or the whole time, or as investors in the project — to make this not only a habitable place, but as a resort equaled by none.

Of all Cayce's weird and wonderful accounts of Atlantis, none is more intriguing than his description of a meeting on the lost continent aimed at ridding the land of huge prehistoric beasts that were reproducing in large numbers. The animals were finally wiped out, said the sleeping prophet, by "sending out super-cosmic rays from various central plants."

Cayce's son, Hugh Lynn, once said his father "didn't like to make predictions. He believed in free will, and didn't like to influence people who might be susceptible to suggestion." Certainly, the prophecies were often a by-product of his desire to help others. The future according to Cayce would slip out involuntarily, woven into the fabric of his psychic readings.

For above all, Cayce was a good man who gave his utmost for humanity. Unwilling to profit materially from his psychic intuition, he guided others to riches while he remained poor. "Not self, but others," was his motto. There were times when he didn't even have enough money to buy the family essentials. His wife, Gertrude, whom Cayce called "Mother," believed the answer to their troubles might lie in a reading, and so she encouraged her husband to "sleep" before asking him, "In consideration of the fact that Edgar Cayce is devoting his entire time to the Work, give the reason for his not being able to obtain sufficient financial support for his and his family's material sustenance, and how may he, Edgar Cayce, correct this condition?" Cayce's reply was in keeping with his life of selfless devotion: "Live closer to Him, who giveth all good and perfect gifts, and ask and ye shall receive; knock and it shall be opened unto you. Give and it shall be returned fourfold. There has never been the lack of necessities, neither will there be, so long as adhering to the Lord's way is kept first and foremost." And that's just the way it turned out. Though hard times came and went, the Cayces were always provided for. But unlike many devout Christians, Cayce did not allow his spirituality to smother his personality. As dedicated as he was to his wife and two sons, he enjoyed the company of attractive women, made his own wine and was an incorrigible chain-smoker. "Where I am going there are no cigarettes," he would tell those who questioned his habit.

That Cayce, a Presbyterian Sunday School teacher, was a deeply religious man had far-reaching effects on the Work, as he respectfully called his profession. His God-fearing nature influenced the language of his writings; sprinkled with words such as Ye, Yea, Thy and Hath, they sound positively Biblical at times. While his belief in reincarnation underpinned his philosophy of life, he attributed his powers to the ability to absorb the "Akashic Records." In his words, they contain that which "the individual entity writes upon the skein of Time and Space, through Patience." In plainer language, these records are the psychic trace of past and future events. All time is encompassed by this "Book of Life," as he called it. Cayce always insisted that past, present and future are one. "That as lived today," he said, "is as tomorrow today for today is tomorrow, tomorrow is today."

Inundated with requests for readings — they poured in at the rate of 1,500 a day — Cayce persisted with the Work right through the last war. But the backlog was so large it was like taking a spoon to a slag heap. He was teetering on the brink of nervous exhaustion, yet still he ignored the advice of his own readings that warned he would disintegrate if he "read" more than twice a day. He battled on, expending far too much effort for his failing body, until his nervous system finally collapsed. But the collapse came too late to save him; the sheer momentum of a life of selflessness had carried him over the edge. He died on January 3, 1945, at the age of sixtyseven.

Today, as Cayce foresaw, his work lives on under the guardianship of the Association for Research and Enlightenment, a non-profit organization based in Virginia Beach and committed to spiritual growth, psychic research and the practical use of Cayce's 14,256 recorded readings. Edgar Cayce may no longer be here in the flesh, but his spirit still runs the A.R.E. Not that he won't be back to scrutinize the work of his successors — he's predicted he'll rejoin us in 1998, possibly as "a liberator of the world."

Jeane Dixon: Paradox is personified in America's greatest living prophet.

6 Jeane Dixon

"A greater power than mine has willed it. I only saw it."

Jeane Dixon

The Dixon Paradox

As a child, Jeane Dixon wanted to be either an actress or a nun. Instead, she became America's greatest living prophet, shaping a lifestyle that reflects a curious blending of those early aspirations. She is, for all the apparent contradiction in terms, a devout showwoman. One Jeane Dixon is "Washington's phenomenal seeress," a fast-talking television personality, a world-syndicated horoscope columnist who faces daily avalanches of fan mail, an aging celebrity with dyed hair, lavish jewelery and expensive clothes who's sensitive about her age (she won't tell, and neither will *Who's Who*). The other Jeane Dixon is a teetotaller and non-smoker who has startled people with her angelic resemblance to the Madonna. She's an intensely private person who, despite an overcrowded schedule, labors selflessly for needy children and old folks alike and strives to spread the Christian gospel into as many homes as possible. Every morning, she carries her deeply felt convictions to Mass after rising early to recite the Twenty-Third Psalm from her window.

Born in a Wisconsin village, one of seven offspring of German immigrant parents, Jeane grew up in California after her father, who'd made a fortune in the lumber trade, headed for Santa Rosa and an early retirement. Jeane's psychic talents were apparent from an early age. She would astound her parents' friends by telling them all about themselves, and she once perplexed her mother by asking for "the letter with the black border around it." Her words made no sense until, two weeks later, an envelope edged in black dropped into the mailbox, bearing news of the death in Germany of Jeane's grandfather. At eight years of age, Jeane was taken to a gypsy fortune-teller who lived in a covered wagon outside Santa Rosa. It was an encounter she was to remember for the rest of her life. The gypsy immediately noticed the heavy crisscross of lines on Jeane's hands and told her she would become a great mystic. She rummaged among her belongings and presented Jeane with a crystal ball. "Take it," she said. "One day you will tell others." Young as she was, Jeane realized from that moment she had a distinct calling in life. Since then, she's used a crystal ball to help her concentrate while meditating on the future, and she's even been known to carry it into church.

Her predictions, which usually come to her in times of silence and meditation, are often disseminated in a welter of hot publicity and electronic hoo-hah beamed to the masses via quarterly prediction columns or televized appearances. Several of her forecasts, pronounced well in advance either to individual witnesses or vast audiences, have sent waves of incredulity through the Western world after events turned out the way she said they would. Her most famous prediction was of the assassination of President John F. Kennedy. But she also foresaw the murders of Senator Robert Kennedy, black civil rights leader Martin Luther King and Mahatma Gandhi, India's spiritual statesman, as well as the shooting of Alabama Governor George Wallace and the premature death of Marilyn Monroe.

In December, 1966, Jeane told Jean Stout, wife of the chief of mission operations for the U.S. Office of Manned Space Flight:

> I see a terrible fiery catastrophe . . . and it will cause the astronauts' deaths . . . I sense their souls leaving the capsule in puffs of smoke.

On January 27, 1967, a raging fire consumed American astronauts Grissom, White and Chafee as they tested the Apollo capsule at Cape Kennedy.

On May 14, 1953, she told millions tuned in to NBC television that "a silver ball going into outer space will circle the earth and come back to Russia . . ." In 1957, the Soviets launched into orbit man's first satellite.

As early as 1949, Jeane informed Ivy Baker Priest, a former United States Treasurer, that Richard Nixon would one day be president, a prediction she repeated in 1953. She warned friends not to fly in the same plane as United Nations Secretary-General Dag Hammarskjold in mid-September, 1961. They did well to listen,

An ancient Canadian Indian legend recorded in 1855 tells how a Chippewa prophet had dreamt of the coming of the white man. The prophet, who lived on a promontory on Lake Superior, described "men of strange appearance" with skins "white like snow" who sailed in "wonderfully large canoes which have great white wings like those of a bird." The strangers had sharp knives and "long black tubes which they point at birds and animals."

"The tubes," the prophet told his people, "make a smoke that rises into the air just like the smoke from our pipes. From them come fire and such terrific noise that I was frightened, even in my dream."

Marilyn Monroe's early death came as no surprise to Jeane Dixon.

Before the Chinese occupation of Tibet in 1959, three prophecies were well known among the six million people who live on the "Roof of the World." It had been foretold that the Tibetans would lose their country, that they would regain it and that the present Dalai Lama — fourteenth in a line of priest-kings who ruled Tibet from 1642 until the Chinese takeover — would be the last. "Most probably I am the last," the Dalai Lama, who lives in exile in India, said. "Nothing wrong. When there is no longer any benefit, then naturally the Dalai Lama ceases to be."

for Hammarskjold perished when his aircraft crashed in Northern Rhodesia on September 18.

Sitting under a dryer in a Hollywood salon, Jeane urged a beautiful blonde actress sitting in the next chair not to take a planned flight across the continent. Carole Lombard shrugged off the advice, only to be killed a few days later when her plane crashed in mountainous country.

Jeane's husband Jimmy initially resisted his wife's warning when she begged him not to fly to Chicago. Although Jimmy was determined to take the plane in spite of Jeane's remonstrating, he changed his mind at the airport and took the train instead. He was glad he did. The plane crashed near Chicago, killing all aboard.

In 1946, Jeane forecast — right to the very day — the partition of India on February 20, 1947. An Indian diplomat based in Washington scoffed at the prediction, believing such a development was impossible. On the morning of the appointed day, with not the slightest whiff of partition in the wind, he called her up to tease her about the unfulfilled prophecy. But Jeane was unperturbed. She calmly replied that the day was not yet over. Next morning, as if by pre-ordained arrangement, the papers carried the news that India was being divided.

She predicted, one month in advance, the monster 1964 earthquake in Alaska. And as early as 1944, she declared, "China will go communist and become our greatest trouble. Africa will be our next biggest worry in the foreign field."

There are innumerable examples of her predictions coming true for friends and acquaintances. Marriages, illnesses, deaths, career changes, accidents, horse race winners, a murder-suicide and a house fire . . . Jeane has successfully signaled all these and many, many more. In 1975 she predicted harm would come to her husband. One night, after unsuccessfully pleading with him not to leave the house, she waited nervously by the door for his return. Minutes later, James Dixon — a man who shows his devotion by placing a red rose on his wife's pillow every day — staggered home after a mugging.

President Roosevelt called Jeane to the White House in November, 1944, and in answer to his question, "How much time do I have to finish the work I have to do?" she replied quite candidly: "Six months or less." Her gloomy forecast was accuracy itself. On April 12, 1945, President Roosevelt died in Georgia of a cerebral hemorrhage. A little later that year, Jeane told Winston Churchill that the British electorate would end his reign as prime minister, though he would later be returned to power. "England will never let me down," Churchill retorted gruffly. Nevertheless, Jeane Dixon was right.

But she hasn't always been right, and that serves only to make her refreshingly human. She forecast the Russians would be first to put a man on the moon; she said Fidel Castro would be removed from Cuban leadership years ago; she said the Chinese would provoke a world war in 1958; she predicted victory for the eventual losers of the 1964 British general election. "My symbols are never wrong," is how Jeane explains her misses, "but sometimes I misinterpret them."

As long as there are rumor-mongers, there's always the danger Jeane will be wrong even before she's opened her mouth. In March, 1964, she was besieged by TV commentators and news reporters and faced with hundreds of letters and phone calls from anguished teenagers after word got out she'd predicted the Beatles would die in a plane crash that August. Not until she denied having said any such thing did the furor subside. Another rumor had Jeane foretelling the deaths of up to 8,000 people in the sinking of the man-made island at Montreal's Expo '67. Then there was the tall story that she'd foreseen malevolent Martians landing on Earth to kidnap children and teenage girls, followed by the alarm in June 1969 that all girls with pierced ears would die of a fearful disease. Denials were issued as fast as the wild stories were circulated. Jeane was forced to call a press conference to protest "Not me!" when a prediction of the imminent disappearance of California was falsely attributed to her.

Jeane Dixon has been enjoying celebrity status for more than thirty years. Rich and poor alike have sought her advice. Visiting diplomats are as keen, if not keener, to check in with America's first lady of prediction as they are to pay their respects at the White House. By 1948, mail and telephone messages had reached such unmanageable proportions that husband Jimmy, owner of Washington's James L. Dixon realty company, decided to offer Jeane a job in his office. Knowing she found it difficult to turn away requests for guidance, he believed a desk job would shield her from the masses in need of counsel and give her a legitimate excuse for not succumbing to every plea. Of course, the mail still poured in from all over the world, some of it addressed simply "Jeane Dixon, U.S.A."

Winston Churchill said, "You know, I always avoid prophesying beforehand. It is much better policy to prophesy after the event has already taken place."

Today, in spite of the pressure exerted each week by hundreds of phone calls and letters, the preparation of her syndicated column, sundry writing projects, TV and radio interviews, speaking engagements and various charitable works, Jeane still holds the job of secretary-treasurer in her husband's firm. Evidently, local house-hunters are far easier to handle than her millions of admirers. As well as being a natural psychic, she's a natural businesswoman. Tapping a powerhouse of nervous energy, she labors twelve hours a day, seven days a week. She loves her work so much she's often said it's a shame God didn't grant her a twenty-hour working day. "I really don't know where she gets the energy," confided her secretary, Linda Roberts. "She wears me out!" Jeane loves talking almost as much as she loves working. She rattles off opinions and anecdotes at a speed that defies the swiftest of note-takers.

The Kennedy Predictions

The source material of Jeane's predictions can be divided roughly into two groups: the revelations (which, she says, are visions of unavoidable events shaping world destiny) and the perceptions, which foreshadow happenings that don't *have* to take place. The revelations are fewer in number but infinitely greater in scope and importance. "All of my revelations deal with international situations," she says. "They are never intended for one person as an individual."

Her prediction of John Kennedy's death was most definitely a revelation. Eleven years before Kennedy was shot in Dallas, Jeane experienced a pressing feeling of expectation for several days; such feelings always precede her most dramatic revelations. This one materialized after she walked into St. Matthew's Cathedral in Washington on a dreary, drizzly morning and stood in front of the statue of the Virgin Mary. Suddenly, a shimmering image of the White House appeared and the numbers 1-9-6-0 formed over the roof, only to be obliterated by a dark cloud that dripped onto the dome. In front of the main door stood the young Kennedy. She watched him steadily as an inner voice told her he would become president of the United States in 1960 and would be assassinated while in office.

The vision stayed with Jeane, and Kennedy's election in 1960 reinforced what she'd learned. As the fateful day closed in, she vainly tried to warn the President that his life was threatened. In Kennedy's last few hours, Jeane was horrifyingly aware that the

John F. Kennedy. Jeane Dixon predicted his death eleven years before he was struck down by an assassin's bullet.

death blow was imminent. She lost her appetite, she paced her office and muttered distracted comments to friends who either told her not to think such thoughts or blankly returned her helplessness with their own. And then — at 12:30 p.m. on November 22, 1963 — the fatal shots were fired. What Jeane Dixon in her heart of hearts knew was inevitable had happened. She has since said that more than one person was responsible for the assassination and that this will eventually become public knowledge.

The killing of Robert Kennedy, Jeane insists, could have been avoided. Again, believing his life was in danger, she tried to alert the youthful Senator and this time the message got through. But the warning made no difference. On May 28, 1968, as Jeane addressed a convention in the grand ballroom of the Ambassador Hotel in Los Angeles, she became aware that deathly omens stalked the halls of the building. As she left the ballroom she sensed a strong foreboding of murder and told friends she was walking over the spot where Kennedy would be assassinated. Warning phone calls were hastily made to Rose Kennedy, the Senator's mother, but they were not returned. A week later, Robert Kennedy was gunned down by Sirhan Bishara Sirhan at the Ambassador Hotel.

"When asked to explain my gift for seeing the future," Jeane Dixon has been quoted as saying, "I tell my questioners that I could no more explain it than I could define love or electricity. And when asked to explain why I am a prophet only of doom, I say this is not so. I make many predictions of happy events for people — but these don't make the headlines." Fair enough. Yet many of Jeane's predictions for the next fifty years are anything but jolly. Take a look at these:

- A comet will strike the earth in the middle of the 1980s, causing potentially disastrous earthquakes and tidal waves.
- Many will "die like ants" in the 1980s as a result of germ warfare unleashed on the Western world by Red China in alliance with Asian and African nations.
- The White House flag will fly at half mast in 1983.
- Changes in doctrine and tradition will cause the Roman Catholic Church to splinter into factions within ten years. The papacy will be seriously weakened by a transfer of power to the cardinals. By the end of this century, one pope will suffer bodily harm and another will be assassinated.
- The Antichrist, whom Jeane says was born in the Middle East on February 5, 1962, will grow up to revolutionize the world with false and seductive teachings. Backed heavily by the United States, he will gain a reputation as a peacemaker but will finally plunge the West into war against Red China in the 2030s.
- Widespread geological upheavals and geographical changes will take place by the end of the century. "Where water is now there will be land, and where there is land today, wild, swirling water will rush in and destroy everything in its path."
- The false security of so-called disarmament will suddenly be broken by world war in 1999.
- Red China's war of conquest against Russia and Russia's satellite states will last from 2020 until 2037.
- A stolen nuclear weapon will terrify an entire continent in 1981. The weapon will be recovered, but not before giving us all a deadly warning of impending disaster.

- More than a dozen African nations will take sides in a great war on that continent in 1987 — the African equivalent of World War Two.
- In 1985, a third Indochina war will break out — the most ruinous of all the armed struggles in that region this century.
- Mexico, with its newly discovered oil wealth, will be plunged into the same kind of social turmoil and political disruption that has afflicted Iran. This should happen in 1987.

More optimistically, however, Jeane Dixon also predicts:

- The world will not end for at least another 3,000 years.
- Soviet writer Alexander Solzhenitsyn will do his greatest work now that he's living in the United States. He will become the central focus of an international movement to restore religious faith to millions. Russia will be converted.
- Intelligent life will be discovered on a sister planet "exactly on the other side of the sun." We will land instruments on Jupiter granting us "a bird's eye view."
- The United States will have its first woman president in the 1980s.
- By the century's end, Canada and Brazil will be among the world's most powerful nations because of their food and energy resources.
- Creatures long thought to be extinct will be found to be still living.
- There will be peace at last in Northern Ireland in 1988.
- By the end of the century, world hunger will have been all but obliterated.
- Icebergs will be towed from the polar zones for commercial use, starting in 1985.
- Australia, Canada and New Zealand will form an international union in the 1990s.

The Antichrist

According to Jeane Dixon, her sinister vision of the coming of the Antichrist is another revelation of an unavoidable, world-shaking event. Her vision allowed her a glimpse of the babe of evil dispensation who, she believes, is now a young man living somewhere in the Middle East. He will imitate Christ's lifestyle and philosophy, expanding his influence with the help of a dedicated band of followers and deceiving the world by carefully veiling his satanic mission. Youth will flock to his side and the propaganda machine of the United States will be used to promote the glory of his name. In her book, *My Life and Prophecies*, Jeane describes how the world will be dominated by the man she sees as "the last and greatest of idols man has worshipped in the long history of religious aberrations." She says:

> The Antichrist will be a phenomenon of the political order. He is not simply a religious "heretic" whom the world at large could simply ignore. No! He will hold earthly power in his hands and use it as his instrument. All the tyrants in history are mere children in comparison with him.
>
> This means first of all that he will be a military figure beyond anything the world has previously seen. He will conquer the whole earth and hold it in complete mastery with the most modern weapons. He will rule his new World Empire with the utmost of military might and glory.

Only divine intervention, it seems, can save the peoples of the world from such subjection. And Jeane prophesies just that — in

Disgraced ex-President Richard Nixon. Jeane Dixon spoke of his "excellent vibrations."

Jerusalem. "That's a revelation I haven't told," she's quoted as saying. "People are not ready for it yet." But she has disclosed that just before the second coming of Christ, "We will all witness the shadow of the cross, the tremor of the earth and three days of darkness."

There's little middle ground when it comes to Jeane Dixon. People either believe her or laugh at her blueprint for the future, dismissing her past, proven predictions as grandly orchestrated flukes. Some even say she's inspired by the devil, that she's a demonic wolf in sheep's clothing. Those daring to question the source of her inspiration point cynically to her uncritical attitude toward President Richard Nixon. Before Watergate, she talked of Nixon's "excellent vibrations" for the good of America. And after the scandal had rocked the nation and forced Nixon's resignation, she was saying unborn historians would one day describe Nixon as "a great president." One thing Jeane Dixon is *not* is a reed shaken by the wind of popular opinion. She still maintains the ex-President's critics will "find that the price the world is paying for trying to discredit Nixon is going to be that we'll practically lose our freedom."

As much as possible, Jeane works at supervising, promoting and sponsoring Children to Children, Inc., the organization she founded in 1964 to help children spiritually, mentally and physically. Money from her speaking engagements goes straight into Children to Children funds. Jeane won't accept a penny for any readings she gives, and much of her secretary's energy is devoted to returning contributions. "Whatever power I have was given to me to be used for others, and can be taken from me if it is misused," she says. Jeane is generous to individuals as well as to charitable organizations; she gave a $10 tip to Toronto make-up artist Elaine Saunders after being prepared for a Canadian television show in May, 1977. "It's most unusual to be given a tip at all," said Mrs. Saunders. "It's funny, though," she added. "As kind and chatty as Jeane Dixon was, she seemed kind of distant. She seemed to be in another world." Jeane has said the same thing about herself. "I see people around me," she once remarked. "They're there and yet they're not there."

The socialite who withdraws; the money-spinner who gives and sacrifices. Although very much of this world, she aspires to a spirituality most of us couldn't emulate even in our dreams. All at once, Jeane Dixon puts on a show and quietly does the deed. All at once, she's the actress and the nun.

"God revealed to me that the United States are destined one day to inherit all the power and prosperity which Great Britain now possesses."—from the 1885 diary of Louis Riel, Canadian native leader of the Métis and self-proclaimed prophet of the New World.

The modern psychics who made predictions especially for this book. From left: Sandra McNeil of Los Angeles, Britain's Simon Alexander and Irene Hughes, America's self-proclaimed first lady of the parasciences.

7 The Modern Psychics

"Better, of course, if images were plain,
   Warnings clearly said, shapes put down quite still
Within the fingers' reach, or else nowhere . . ."

Kingsley Amis

The "Sensitives"

Whether they like it or not, the psychics are the ones the future has chosen. They are walking antennae; they are highly sensitive receivers crackling with broadcasts of events to come. Sometimes the broadcasts are transmitted with studio clarity, sometimes static overwhelms the word and drowns the message and sometimes the airwaves are crowded with cacophony. That's where the trouble lies. Some psychics are more tuned in than others, but they all have the same difficulty determining whether they've picked up the Voice of Tomorrow or just gibberish.

All the same, when they *think* they've latched onto something important, they turn it over to the public as a prediction. Sometimes they're right; more frequently, they are wrong. But when the same message is received by a number of psychics — as before the assassinations of the Kennedy brothers — there's a better than average chance the predicted event will become reality. We've matched the countless predictions of the long-range psychics and selected those forecasts that cropped up with the greatest frequency. Here is a sampling of what we can expect over the next twenty years:

- Space exploration will flourish. We will make contact with beings from outer space and learn where UFOs come from.
- Medical science will be revolutionized and major breakthroughs made in the treatment of cancer, cerebral palsy and muscular dystrophy.
- Devastating volcanoes and earthquakes will change the face of the world. California will be among the worst hit areas.

- Some form of nuclear war will break out within ten years.
- A United States president will die in office in the 1980s.
- New York will be destroyed.
- Great advances will be made in psychic research and greater use made of psychic perception in everyday life.

The dictionary describes psychics as people who are ''specially sensitive to influences or forces of a non-physical, apparently supernatural nature.'' Although all of us are said to possess latent psychic powers, psychic ability is neither chosen nor attained. It simply happens. When asked to explain their insights, the psychics are unable to find words to convey what they are experiencing. All they can say is that their predictions are usually dreamed, heard or felt, materializing sometimes as a mixture of all three sensations.

Psychics have always been part of society, and often in past days they were persecuted for their gifts. Looking into the future was considered usurping God's power, and people feared them as mem-

Calgary in winter: shades of the coming ice age forecast by Irene Hughes?

bers of the Devil's legions. Today, however, we're somewhat more tolerant; we cultivate the psychics while laughing at many of their predictions. They themselves range from housewives to psychiatrists, from laborers to ministers of religion, and their experiences are just as varied. Says Britain's top clairvoyant and former north country hairdresser Simon Alexander, "It's like a movie camera in my mind. I project the pictures on a wall or a blank piece of paper. Them's my crystal ball. The pictures intrude most powerfully when I'm lying awake in bed. It's terribly harrowing. So I sleep with the light on, and that helps dim my vision." Jamaican psychic Dr. Ernesto Montgomery — who says he's been "bombarded" by visions of a California earthquake that will strike at 2:30 a.m. on July 15, 1983 and kill more than 18 million people — has tiny appendages behind his ears which hurt before a psychic vision. "Doctors are as baffled as I am as to why they are there or how they operate," he says.

Though psychics have always been with us, their mysterious gifts are only today gaining some measure of acceptance and respectability. Growing numbers of scientific researchers are beginning to investigate the phenomenon of foresight. The late Dr. Alexis Carrel, physiologist, biologist and Nobel Prize winner, did much to encourage this trend when he said, "The facts of prediction of the future lead us to the threshold of an unseen world. They seem to point to the existence of a psychic principle capable of evolving outside the limits of our bodies." French writer Jules Romains put the case for the Unknown even more strongly in *I Believe* when he wrote, "Once the most important results of psychic experimentation are proved and officially recognized as 'truths,' positive science will be challenged within its own province." Paul Neary, a New York psychic, says research is advancing so rapidly that by 1990, psychics will be employed to heal mental illness. Former actress Kebrina Kinkade predicts that by the turn of the century, psychics will be used for espionage and accepted as expert witnesses in courtrooms. Tenny Hale, Oregon's top-rated psychic, expects law enforcement to be conducted by psychic means, and Baptist minister David Bubar believes psychics will hold important government posts by 1990.

The Psychics Predict . . .

Meanwhile, the "sensitives" at the beck of Beyond are happy to churn out predictions that are fed to an eager public by newspapers, magazines and television. The big names have become famous by

A Cornish farmer's weather predictions based on the activities of local gnats entertained the British public in 1947. Newspapers ran a scoreboard showing how the farmer fared in comparison with the meteorologists. For several weeks, his natty forecasts proved far more successful than those of the professionals!

In July, 1979, as India's Charan Singh prepared to battle for power in the world's largest democracy, his fortune-teller told him, "Make your moves between the 7th. and the 17th., to bear fruit on the 27th."

Sound advice it was, because defections from Morarji Desai's Janata government began after the 7th and by the 17th. Charan Singh had quit as deputy premier and been unanimously elected leader of the breakaway Janata (Secular) Party. Shortly afterward, the government collapsed. On the 27th, Singh became prime minister, announcing, "Now I have achieved my life's ambition."

Oh, perfidious predictor! There wasn't a word in the reading that a mere twenty-four days later, victory and power would be snatched away when his administration suddenly broke down.

scoring a few dramatic hits, but at times they've all been very wrong. We remember the successes and tend to forget the failures, perhaps because we have a need to believe. Sir Francis Bacon's observation three centuries ago that "men never mark when they miss" is as true today as it was then. What fascinates us is that we can never be sure one way or the other until either the event occurs or the allotted span has gone by. Predictions have all the allure, although none of the prize money, of a lottery.

Because so many predictions by modern psychics are tiresome variations on the same old themes, we're including just a sprinkling from the flood. We start our selection with Chicago's Irene Hughes, America's self-proclaimed first lady of the parasciences. She made the following predictions especially for this book:

- An oncoming ice age will be "very evident" by 1983 and fully upon us by 1989.
- Missouri, Kentucky and Tennessee will suffer from terrible earthquakes in 1981 and 1982. On or very near March 10, 1986, a giant quake will rock San Francisco.
- The world will be on the verge of nuclear war in 1983. China will stir up Africa and other nations against the United States, and in 1985 sophisticated nuclear weapons small enough to tuck into a pocket will be used in the conflict which "will not be an all-out destructive war."
- Quebec will secede from Canada no later than 1985.
- Queen Elizabeth will abdicate and Prince Charles will take over the throne for about three years, then step down. Illness will cause the Queen's abdication.
- Paris will be burned to the ground before 2000, Italy will suffer famine and destructive earthquakes between 1983 and 1989 and Rome will be destroyed shortly after 2000.
- The next pope will be assassinated and cardinals will rule the Church until the papacy is no more in 1989.

We asked Simon Alexander, who successfully predicted the 1979 Tory election victories in Britain and Canada and foretold — to the hour — the final split between Richard Burton and Liz Taylor, to focus his psychic "eye" on the year 2000. This is what he saw.

The world will be beset by racial problems. The greatest threat will come from China "which has sapped the resources of every major nation under the guise of friendship." China will ally itself with the group of countries known as the "Minorities" — comprised mainly of black nations — which will push the world toward conflict. Russia, however, will practically be a friend of the West. Racked by internal problems, the Soviet Union will have to westernize to keep the masses happy. Russia will no longer be red, more "a fine shade of pink." Open political elections will be held there.

Five countries will be at war in Africa and a NATO force will take sides in the struggle. A "stupid American president" will commit Canadian troops to the conflict. Indeed, Canada will lose much of its identity through political and economic entanglement with its mighty neighbor to the south. The Americans will "con" Canadians into building too many nuclear plants and the people of Canada will feel they are "sitting on a time bomb," as there will already have been, in the late 1980s, a nuclear disaster in the States which wiped out an entire community. Many Canadians will emigrate to Australia.

Ireland will be united, the IRA having lost the power to terrorize,

The British royals. Illness will cause the Queen's abdication, and Charles will take over — but not for long.

Wall Street speculator · Frederick N. Goldsmith predicted stock market gains with the help of a comic strip in one of the American daily newspapers. While others merely laughed at the cartoon characters' antics, Goldsmith consulted the comics for their hidden meaning, the key to which had been passed on to him by the spirit of a dead investor. More than ninety per cent of his tips were said to be profitable and subscribers to Goldsmith's circular letter paid $25 for the privilege of sharing his insights. For fifty years Goldsmith raked in an annual income of $39,000 until, in 1948, the authorities caught up with the source of the eighty-three year old's inspired forecasting and charged him with "misrepresentation."

and Greece will be the major European troublespot. South Africa will cease to exist. Israel will be a nation in name only, having been deserted by its powerful allies. Most of Israel will be controlled by Arab nations, but strife and struggle in the Middle East will continue.

Great Britain will be led by a right wing government and be most unpopular with the rest of the world. Large-scale expulsion of immigrants will take place and class distinction will be more pronounced than ever. The death penalty will be re-instated and the National Health system dismantled. Nevertheless, the pound will be "very strong." Both the Canadian and Australian dollars will rank among the most durable currencies, but the American dollar will falter.

Catholicism will lose its hold on the traditionally Catholic countries, largely through the Vatican's stand on contraception and priesthood celibacy. Pornography will be a thing of the past. Exploited sex will not be at all popular, with great stress laid on the natural integration of sexual attitudes. The body will be "much more covered."

And finally, no "super civilization" will be discovered on other planets, but contact will be made with a backward, humanoid form of life.

Sandra McNeil of Los Angeles, the most glamorous of the modern psychics, specializes in predicting medical and scientific breakthroughs. For this book, she forecasts:

- As early as 1981, robots will be used in the home, not only as messengers, cooks and cleaners, but also as companions. By 2000, computer robots will be introduced in the classroom as "teachers' aids."
- A wrist device to inform diabetics of blood-sugar levels will be on the market shortly. This will be followed, in 1981, by an injection that will arrest diabetes for fifty years.
- A serum that prevents hardening of the arteries and reverses senility and the aging process will become available in the 1980s. By 2000, average life expectancy will be increased to 120 years.
- Synthetic repair will provide a cure for heart disease by 1993. The 1990s will see cures for arthritis, cancer and multiple sclerosis.
- By 1990 a device will have been invented to enable us to communicate with plants. A computer analyzer will translate a plant's vibrations into human voice.

- Hypnosis and "conditioning tapes" will be used in schools by the turn of the century. These programming techniques will make it possible for physics, languages, astronomy and calculus to be taught to pre-schoolers.
- By 1987-88, airplanes will cross the Atlantic Ocean in less than twenty-five minutes.
- By 1990, there will be proof of life in outer space when a Russian mission encounters and "captures" an organism from another planet.
- The United States will establish an experimental space station in the early 1990s that will house several hundred people for over a year. Volunteers will undergo special training to take part in the project.

Ross Peterson of Flint, Michigan has been hailed as the new Edgar Cayce. Like Cayce, he gives his predictions in a self-induced trance and has much to say about geological upheaval. Peterson forecasts the earth's crust will begin its transformation in Georgia and the Carolinas, to be followed, in 1989 or 1990, by disastrous West Coast earthquakes that will submerge California. By 2006 New York, too, will sink into the sea, and in 2030 large portions of Europe will vanish "as in the batting of an eye" — a choice of words echoing Cayce's prediction that northern Europe will change "in the twinkling of an eye." Peterson says Spain, Portugal, parts of Italy, Ireland and the west coast of Britain will disappear under the waves. All this catastrophic activity will serve to lead mankind back to religion, and Peterson foresees Russia reverting to a modified form of Christianity and Asia experiencing great spiritual re-birth.

Maha Yogi A.S. ("My friends call me 'Alf'") Narayana is the Berlin-born president of the Toronto-based Espon Corporation which sells his psychic services to individuals and companies. Claiming at least ninety per cent accuracy, the impeccably groomed Yogi charges $3,000 per typewritten page and demands a downpayment of $10,000 for overseas assignments. But he warns of an "error factor" of twenty-five per cent in his public, not-for-profit predictions, just so his paying customers won't feel hard done by. Here are some of the Yogi's "public" predictions:

- A new Watergate involving close to $17 million is in the making in the United States.
- By 1985, all the world's dictators will either be dead or in hiding on obscure islands.

Being a predictor had its drawbacks for Basil Shackleton.

"Sometimes," said the London photographer in 1944, "I sit in a bar having a drink and for no apparent reason a complete stranger will grab me by the neck and punch me in the jaw."

Shackleton — the man who, in 1940, forecast the war in Europe would end on August 17, 1945 (he was 100 days off) — believed he kept on being thumped because his powerful, probing mind disturbed those with lesser equipment. His attackers, he reasoned, were responding instinctively to aggravating thought waves.

Psychic predictor Criswell says the world will end on August 18, 1999 when a magnetic disturbance will deprive Earth of its oxygen. The planet will be jolted from its orbit and race toward the sun, leaving a handful of humans on 200 space stations to fend for themselves.

- The United States of North and Central America will be founded within five years.
- The Japanese economy will break down between 1980 and 1984.
- Pierre Trudeau will be appointed to a top-ranking post in the United Nations by 1982.
- Bad harvests in the Soviet Union between 1980 and 1987 will help reduce that country to a second-rate power.
- A world state, using a currency "something like the kilowatt," is less than ten years away.

Former mortician Criswell is both prolific and far-fetched, but not without success. Nor is he without his share of blunders, for that matter. He was wrong in predicting Blacks led by a man called Sanders would take over Mississippi by 1973 and establish a model state. And the vicious ice storms he said would kill 5,000 people in New Hampshire in the winter of 1974 never materialized. But he scored in anticipating the Arab-Israeli Six Day War in June, 1967 and the deaths of Jayne Mansfield and Martin Luther King. If Criswell's future is to be believed, we have some crazy times to look forward to. His prognostications span the legalization of polygamy in North Dakota in 1985, the near-destruction of London by a falling meteor on October 18, 1988, a woman called the Lady of Light becoming, in 1985, the leader of the Orient and then of the world and the women of St. Louis losing their hair between February 11 and May 11, 1983. From May, 1988 until March, 1989, Criswell says the American population will become sex-crazed after an aphrodisiac is pumped into water and heating systems across the nation.

Dr. N., an anonymous physician and psychiatrist from California, says that by 1986 one in three children will be deformed by radiation, and that by 1987 people will be routinely tested for cancer every six months. Fortunately, the enigmatic Dr. N. was wrong in predicting the United States and China would be at war by 1972, a war in which radioactive fall-out would kill 190 million Chinese and render the West Coast states uninhabitable.

Kathy Sotka, a psychic research counselor at the Midwestern Institute of Parapsychology, accurately predicted the massive earthquake that killed over 655,000 people in China in 1976, but erred in forecasting Edward Kennedy would be elected president that year. She sees ocean farming becoming a most popular and profitable venture by 1986. Around the same time, the "fountain of youth" will be discovered through mind power and pyramid energy rather than through chemicals. By 1990, fashions will have reverted to the grace and glory of ancient Greece and Rome.

English psychic Frederick Davies foresees a manned landing on Mars between 1983 and 1985 and says we'll have found life on Jupiter and communicated with other planets by 1990. Sicilian-born hairdresser Joseph DeLouise of Chicago has proved himself as a disaster prophet by successfully predicting a Virginia bridge collapse that killed forty-six people, a train crash south of Chicago, a plane crash near Indianapolis and upsets in space for both Russian and American astronauts. In the next few years he expects Japan to merge with China and the British to dispense with the monarchy at the end of Queen Elizabeth's reign.

The IRA killing of Lord Mountbatten on August 27, 1979 fulfilled a prediction made months earlier by Margaret Blake Booth, a Christian Spiritualist from Toronto, that the Royal Family would experience tragedy during the year. Looking ahead, she says Prince Charles will have two children, UFOs will send signals to a South American lookout station and Prince Andrew will marry a Canadian of Anglo-Saxon background and become Governor General of Canada.

Alan Vaughan, who wrote in *Patterns of Prophecy* (1973) that predictions about particular persons "are much more likely to be fulfilled than the prophecies of general events," offers, nevertheless, the general predictions that America will go to war with China in 1981 and that a great new religion combining Christianity with other religions will be introduced during the century's last decade.

By 1990, says Swedish psychic Olof Jonsson, all major cities will have banned private cars while Ann Jensen, a crystal-gazer from Dallas, Texas, says she sees "a woman at the head of world government" between 1991 and 2000. Daniel Logan, who lives in New York State's Catskill Mountains, predicts the Pope will reveal secret information about Christ between 1983 and 1987, and that superior beings from outer space will teach us how to solve the energy crisis by 1996.

While the messages of most latter-day seers of the West can be read and enjoyed with a certain levity, the words of Gopi Krishna demand an altogether more serious approach. Krishna, an Indian prophet who maintains that a mystical element called life-energy or Prana is the "one unalterable precondition" for all psychic phenomena, writes at length in *The Shape of Events to Come* (1979) of the inevitability of nuclear war. Born in Kashmir in 1903, Krishna expresses himself in a rhyming style reminiscent of Nostradamus.

Alaska will be known as the crossroads of the world within fifty years, says Kentucky psychic David Hoy. An "earth capital" may be built there.

Gopi Krishna. Appalling horror followed by "a One-World State built on the Golden Mean."

He says he pens his verses "like a pupil taught by silent whispers coming out of naught." These whispers conjure up a hellish vision of world nations lusting after power and wealth and eventually destroying one another in a "mad race for supremacy." No dates are given for the prophecies (though an aide disclosed Krishna expects them to be fulfilled by the turn of the century), but the warning is that we are already fearfully close to turning the earth "into one vast, rotating urn." He describes his vision this way:

As with eyes open and the mind awake
I am allowed to watch scene after scene
Of stark, appalling horror that will make
The blooming earth, now lovely and serene,
A foul inferno, glowing red in space . . .

Whole towns will vanish or in ruins lie,
And deserts burn where crowded cities were,
Millions with hunger, thirst or terror die,
And millions run round shrieking mad with fear.
Millions disfigured, crippled, wounded, maimed,
Tortured at every step, would limp and crawl
Their faces pale with anguish, eyes inflamed,
With hardship or exhaustion dead to fall.
Men, women, children, sick, infirm and weak
Dishevelled, sleepless, hungry, plagued by flies,
Too ill to drive them off, to move or speak,
In vain will look for help till their hope dies.

But like so many prophets of doom, Krishna offers final hope. After man has been plunged into the inferno and the "Lesson" learned, there dawns a new age of enlightenment. He writes:

When dust has settled on the fiery scene,
Then on the ashes of the past would rise
A One-World State built on the Golden Mean
To make man happy, healthy, peaceful, wise.

Victims of Vision

Psychic awareness can be painful and there must be times when the "receivers" of the twentieth century feel as anguished as English visionary Thomas Gray when he wrote more than 200 years ago, "Ye unborn ages crowd not on my soul!" With the exception of those rare individuals who rake in rewards from syndicated columns and television appearances, there's little profit in being a prophet. There's not much fun, either. Nobody wants to hear bad news, but bad news is the psychics' lot because nothing scrapes their sensitivities more than misfortune. Whether they're right or wrong, they have to live with their foreboding until the appointed hour. Should their sixth sense be accurate, they must still suffer the pain the fulfilled prediction brings. And if they are wrong, they must contend with the scoffing of skeptics. Even if they try to keep their unpleasant messages to themselves, they stand to be pilloried for withholding information that could be used to avert tragedy. That's the psychics' dilemma; that's the price they pay for a ''gift'' outside their control and beyond our understanding.

"I predict that the 1980s will see us relieved of the burdens of astrology, flying saucers, Jeane Dixon, the Bermuda Triangle, and other idiocies."
James Randi, magician and investigator of psychic phenomena.

Nuclear warfare, a common prognostication among the modern psychics.

III THE PROFESSIONAL PREDICTORS

For centuries, predictions sprung from mystical sources alone. But gradually philosophers, writers, scientists and, most recently, a new breed of technocrat called the futurist have ventured onto the soothsayers' slippery ground to invest the old art with practical application for the twentieth century. In this section, we look at the development of these most tangible of predictions that have multiplied, as long-range planning — no longer merely desirable — has become fundamental to our survival. After engaging the predictors' scientific and social forecasts, we consider the futurists' designs on Tomorrow.

Verne came close to naming
the Cape Kennedy launch
site. He picked "Tampa
Town," 123 miles away.

8 Science as Prophecy

"When a distinguished but elderly scientist states that something is possible, he is almost certainly right. When he states that something is impossible, he is very probably wrong."

Arthur C. Clarke

The Primacy of Imagination

Space prophet Arthur C. Clarke believes a powerful, flexible imagination is much more valuable than specialized knowledge when it comes to making scientific predictions. No one bears this out better than the Franciscan monk Roger Bacon (1220-1292). Back in the days when science was just something to dream about, he had nothing *but* his imagination to work with. Yet his imaginings soared above the feudal preoccupations of the Dark Ages; somehow he managed to look beyond the suit of armor as the pinnacle of contemporary accomplishment. He wrote:

> Instruments may be made by which the largest ships, with only one man guiding them, will be carried with greater velocity than if they were full of sailors. Chariots may be constructed that will move with incredible rapidity without the help of animals. Instruments of flying may be formed in which a man, sitting at his ease and meditating in any subject, may beat the air with his artificial wings after the manner of birds . . . as also machines which enable men to walk at the bottom of the seas . . .

Two hundred and fifty years before the Portuguese explorer Ferdinand Magellan led his round-the-world expedition, Bacon suggested this voyage was possible. He also foresaw the invention of spectacles and "bridges across rivers without piers or other supports." And he described technological developments that sound far-fetched even to us. He talks about a pocket anti-gravity device as well as the "easy" task of producing a powerful magnetic machine that would work on human beings:

"They will never try to steal the phonograph. It is not of any commercial value."

Thomas Edison (1847-1931)

"Landing and moving around on the moon offers so many serious problems for human beings that it may take science another two hundred years to lick them."

Reader's Digest, 1948

The most crabby technological prediction we could find comes from the lips of astronomer A.W. Bickerton. In 1926, he said, "This foolish idea of shooting at the moon is an example of the absurd length to which vicious specialization will carry scientists working in thought-tight compartments."

. . . by a machine three fingers high and wide and of less size a man could free himself and his friends from all danger of prison and rise and descend. Also a machine can easily be made by which one man can draw a thousand to himself by violence against their wills, and attract other things in like manner.

Hurdling 700 years of scientific progress with sheer imagination puts Bacon in a class by himself; his achievement makes the efforts of some of his successors look pretty pathetic. Many predictors since the Industrial Revolution have erred disastrously in basing their speculations on what they considered to be the most reliable source: their own knowledge. To his everlasting embarrassment, mathematician-astronomer Simon Newcomb (1839-1909) ruled out the airplane by saying: "No possible combination of known forms of machinery and known forms of force, can be united in a practical machine by which men shall fly long distances through the air." Venerable sci-fi author H.G. Wells hastily abandoned the idea of submarines. "I must confess," he said in 1902, "that my imagination . . . refuses to see any sort of submarine doing anything but suffocate its crew and founder at sea." Engineer N.S. Norway (who later wrote novels under the pen name of Neville Shute) was much too timid when he attempted to predict the state of aircraft development fifty years on. By 1980, he said in 1929, airplanes would have a range of 600 miles and be able to achieve speeds of up to 130 miles an hour. How he would have marveled at the Concorde airliner that in 1978 could travel more than 3,000 miles at speeds of over 1,300 miles an hour! J.W. Campbell, an astronomer at the University of Alberta, wrote a paper in 1938 claiming that rocket flight to the moon "now seems less remote than television appeared 100 years ago." Campbell argued that one million tons of fuel would be required to lift a one pound satellite into orbit. But today, less than one ton is needed to shoot one pound into orbit. Even more short-sighted, however, was Britain's Astronomer Royal Richard van der Riet Wooley who, in 1956, declared: "Space travel is utter bilge." Within months the Russians had launched Sputnik, and it became obvious how hollow Wooley's words really were. Some predictors are better than others and some ages are more conducive to prophecy than others. But these examples testify to more than the awesome progress of science; they show that anyone who intends to make a prediction had best beware lest his imagination fail.

John Napier (1550-1617), the Scottish inventor of logarithmic tables and the decimal point, predicted a cannon shell that would destroy all life within a radius of one mile. Today, only a nuclear warhead of at least five kilotons can wreak such destruction.

The wonders — and the horrors, too — of the Industrial Revolution revealed the boundless scope of man the engineer. Suddenly, the walls were down. The potential for technological advancement was as endless as space itself, and a new form of writing emerged to express this sense of exploration: science-fiction. As know-how grew in range and sophistication, so did scientific fantasy. The world was up for grabs. Excitement attended every far-fetched scenario, every Utopian design. Everything seemed possible. Since World War Two, many of the possibilities have become probabilities, if not certainties. As engineer-inventor Buckminster Fuller said in 1966, "It is all Buck Rogers — and it will happen." Yet how much more difficult it must have been to conjure up visions of technological advancement *before* the age of technology. Having touched upon Bacon's foresight, let's look at the predictions of the grand old master of invention, Leonardo da Vinci.

Technology's Ancestors

Da Vinci (1452-1519) had an insatiable hunger for knowledge. Driven by the urgings of his imagination, he strove incessantly for new ideas and insights. He explained his restlessness this way: "Iron rusts from disuse, stagnant water loses its purity, and in cold weather

More than any one man, Leonardo da Vinci epitomizes the spirit of foresight in science.

becomes frozen; even so does inaction sap the vigors of the mind.'' While studying art in Florence, he started the diary that was to serve as the foundation of his life's work. He took stacks of notes, but fearing plagiarism — shades of the industrial theft prevalent today! — he jotted them down in a kind of code. Exploring subjects as diverse as anatomy, sculpture, engineering and physics, he used his artistic talent to sketch complex mechanical devices, many of which were not to be produced for another several hundred years. His designs were his predictions.

Da Vinci's studies taught him that a flexible wing could be built to simulate the motion of birds in flight. In the late nineteenth century, several foolhardy types tried to emulate his idea by building and wearing sets of wings like those in the maestro's blueprints. These would-be flyers can be seen in old movies plummeting to earth from London Bridge or the Eiffel Tower. But it wasn't until Rogallo developed his para-glider for NASA in the early 1960s that da Vinci's concept came close to realization.

Many of da Vinci's ideas were mechanically perfect, but they couldn't be developed because the necessary motive power was lacking. He didn't even have steam at his disposal, so pure muscle had to be used. Inspiration came from a variety of sources. His design for a military tank, for example, answered a defence request from an Italian province about to be attacked by a rival dukedom. The large wooden ''mole'' had cannons protruding from sloping sides designed to deflect cannonballs. He described his contraption this way:

> . . . the tank takes the place of elephants, one may tilt with them. One may hold bellows in them to spread terror among the horses of the enemy, and one may put carabineers in them to break up every company.

Other inventions of the future from da Vinci's drawing board included:

- A machine gun with ten barrels, able to be fired simultaneously or individually. Its breech-loading and screw elevation were two features not to be incorporated for another 300 years.
- Projectiles. Fabricated from metal rather than the stone of his day, they resembled modern military shells.
- A two-level bridge with the top level for pedestrians, similar to those in vogue in the last century. He also designed a rotating bridge.

- Gear systems. His clock designs had two sets of gears, one for hours and one for minutes. Clocks with minute hands, which first appeared in the seventeenth century, were unheard of in da Vinci's day.
- Materials testing rig. Just as automotive and aircraft engineers build test rigs to evaluate the performance of various engineering components, so da Vinci used them to test the breaking strength of wire.
- Jack. Almost identical to those supplied with today's cars, complete with reversing ratchet.
- Odometer. Put to use in da Vinci's extensive mapmaking.

Muscle was the only source of motive power in da Vinci's time. Hence, this man-powered helicopter.

Da Vinci applied his genius to one project after another. Centuries before the invention of aeronautics, he was toiling away on designs for the first parachute (he called it a "tent of linen") and the first helicopter. He was confident man would fly, judging from the instruments he devised: an airspeed indicator and a clinometer for measuring the angle of flight. He also formulated Isaac Newton's laws of motion well over a century before Newton was born. And he even found time to dabble in inventing a way to walk on water that found its way onto the market as a plastic plaything only twenty years ago!

Da Vinci's versatility was matched in a more abstract way by Sir Francis Bacon (1561-1626). One of the greatest minds in English history, Bacon was accomplished as a politician, lawyer, scientist, historian, philosopher, poet and essayist. It's ironic that having made so many predictions that were to be fulfilled, he was so scornful of prophecies. "My judgement is," he sniffed, "that they ought all to be despised; and ought to serve but for winter talk by the fire-side."

Bacon anticipated the era of mass production. In the posthumously published *New Atlantis* (1627), he envisaged buildings for studying what he called "engines of motion" (we call them machines), as well as sound, light and color — the prototypes of our research laboratories. From the findings of these "houses of study," machines would be built to undertake all sorts of projects. From the investigation of sound would come hearing aids and the ability to "convey sound over great distance through tubes." He was talking, of course, about the telephone. From studying light and color, Bacon foresaw "light intensified and thrown great distances." This theme was adopted much later by early twentieth century sci-fi writers like Frank Paul (in his 1929 *Air Wonder* stories), who turned this light

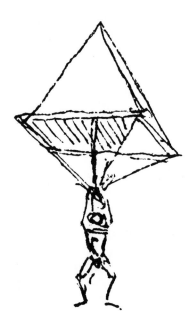

Da Vinci's parachute — or "tent of linen," as he called it. Proof of his belief man would eventually fly.

beam into a weapon of destruction. The laser, as it was to be called, was not developed until the 1960s.

Although Bacon forecast submarines and flying machines, he was more interested in food production and preservation. Modern Israel would not have its substantial produce trade without Bacon's concept of forced multi-crop gardens and hybrid agriculture, or his method of turning salt water into fresh water. He also worked on a proposal for a refrigerator, but lacking the electricity, compressors and freon gas of the modern fridge, he had to be satisfied with plain ice and caves. In fact, Bacon was conducting a frosty experiment to determine whether a chicken stuffed with snow would resist putrefaction when he caught the chill that killed him. He perished a week later, a martyr in the cause of technological advancement.

Time Machines

The first scientifically based predictions of space travel were made by the German astronomer Johannes Kepler early in the seventeenth century. His book *Somnium* (1634) foretells weightlessness and the lack of oxygen in space, as well as the effects of gravitational pull on spaceships. Cyrano de Bergerac, in *A Voyage to the Moon* (1657), was the first to talk of taking a rocket to the moon, even though his rockets were propelled by firecrackers. However, it took the fathers of science-fiction — Jules Verne and H.G. Wells — to make both the man in the street and the scientists aware of the possibilities of space travel. These two writers enthralled their public with technological fairy tales in the late nineteenth century. They had a special talent for dressing up graceless, sometimes ugly, hardware in the frills of fantasy.

In Verne's *From the Earth to the Moon* (1865), the spacecraft, a shiny, snub-nosed aluminum cylinder, is blasted skyward from a tube buried deep in the earth. What seems odd to us is that the astronauts are wearing smoking jackets and reclining on red velvet buttoned couches! So convincing, however, was this story to the readers of the last century that the French author received hundreds of letters from people wanting to sign up for the next moon flight.

Before Verne's introduction of aluminum, the metal had been considered semi-precious; Napoleon was even presented with an aluminum tea service and cutlery set as a novelty. But the hull of Verne's spaceship changed all that, and industry began to introduce many new uses for the metal. Aluminum-frame airships appeared in 1901, and aircraft with aluminum fuselages were first manufactured in 1917. A classic case of the predictor as industrial engineer! The idea of firing the spaceship from a buried gun barrel was adapted by Hitler in the Second World War as a launching pad for his V-3 weapon. Fortunately his "high pressure pumps," as the Führer called them, never surpassed the development stage, but several installations were dug in the limestone plateau of northwestern France, each pointing at England's industrial heartland.

Verne chose "Tampa Town" in Florida for the launching site of his spaceship. "Tampa Town," or plain Tampa as we know it today, is only 123 miles from Cape Kennedy, the blast-off headquarters of the American space program. Verne's tracking telescope was perched on "the summit of Long's Peak in the territory of Missouri,"

Francis Bacon. Though he scoffed at the art of predicting, many of his ideas have been adapted by today's agricultural experts.

Besides possessing a celebrated nose, Cyrano de Bergerac foretold of the time when man would reach the moon.

Author Edward Everett Hale suggested in 1870 that an orbiting brick "moon," 200 feet in diameter, might be used as a navigational aid. And so he predicted the navigation satellites of the United States. He also scored by specifying brick — today, space vehicles are equipped with ceramic nose cones to withstand frictional heat.

whereas NASA's telescopes peer from the mountains of California. In *Round the Moon* (1870), Verne's capsule splashes down in the ocean to be met by a specialized recovery vessel — exactly the method selected by today's space technologists.

The First Men in the Moon (1901) by Englishman H.G. Wells describes the weightlessness not to be experienced by astronauts for another sixty years:

> I perceived an unaccountable change in my bodily sensations. It was a feeling of lightness, of unreality. . . He pointed to the loose cases and bundles that had been lying on the blankets at the bottom of the sphere. I was astonished to see that they were floating nearly a foot from the spherical wall.

Neither Wells nor Verne restricted themselves to space travel. In *The Time Machine* (1895), a mechanical device propels Wells' protagonist through time to the year 2100. He awakes to find himself in a radically altered world. Gone are the rich velour drapes over the windows. Gone is the small cast iron fireplace with its heavy mantlepiece. There he is in a stark white box of a room while, outside, sunlight soaks an unfamiliar landscape. Glossy carriages (without horses, of course) hurtle by at great speed and a distant roar fills the air as a great metal object glides across the sky. Suddenly he hears a voice at his side and he jumps; he didn't hear anyone

A space module as seen by Jules Verne around 1865. Crew number, escape velocity, travel time, re-entry — Verne was amazingly accurate in these and other details.

enter the room. He turns around and there's no one there — only a box with an illuminated window. Strange . . . the voice seems to be trapped inside.

Although the story has since been devoured by movie producers, science continues to scoff at the idea of time travel. Yet recent research has revealed the likelihood of a particle called a tachyon which moves *only* faster than light, confounding the scientists, Einstein included, who stated that *nothing* could move that fast. Time travel just might happen after all.

In *When the Sleeper Wakes* (1899), Wells predicted automatic doors: "A long strip of the apparently-solid wall rolled up with a snap, hung over the two retreating men and fell again . . ." Straying into the realm of social prediction, he also foretold the time when religion would be marketed like soap powder. In the days when churchgoing was characterized by reverence, Wells suggested these jazzy neon slogans to pull in the congregations of the future:

The Apollo mission astronauts on the moon.

American prophet Andrew Jackson Davis predicted both the motor car and the airplane as long ago as 1856.

Of the automobile, he wrote:

Carriages will be moved by a strange and beautiful and simple admixture of aqueous and atmospheric gases — easily condensed, so simply ignited, and so imparted by a machine resembling our [steam] engines, as to be entirely concealed and manageable between the forward wheels.

And of the airplane:
. . . aerial cars . . . will move through the sky from country to country; and their beautiful influence will produce a universal brotherhood of acquaintance.

PUT YOUR MONEY ON THE MAKER
BE A CHRISTIAN — WITHOUT HINDRANCE
    TO YOUR PRESENT OCCUPATION
ALL THE BRIGHTEST BISHOPS ON THE BENCH
    TONIGHT AND PRICES AS USUAL

In Amiens, France in 1875, Jules Verne, who had no scientific training, rattled off a series of predictions in a lecture entitled *In the Twenty-Ninth Century — The Day of an American Journalist.* Technology outdistanced him by 900 years. He mentioned:

- Streets 100 yards wide and buildings 1,000 feet high that are always "of an equable temperature." (New York's Empire State Building, constructed in 1931, is 1,250 feet high and air-conditioned.)
- Cities that "may include up to 10 million inhabitants." (New York's population is about 12 million.)
- Air and underwater trains. "How greatly," said Verne, "would travelers value the aero trains and especially these pneumatic tubes laid beneath the oceans which may convey them with a speed of 1,000 miles an hour." While Sir Freddie Laker's Sky Train shuttle is operating between London and New York, we're still waiting for the deep sea version. Verne also described the sky "furrowed with aero cars and aero buses."
- "Telephonic journalism." Verne's description of a spoken newspaper — our television newscasts.
- Computers. "Bent over their computers," said Verne, "thirty savants were absorbed in equations of the fifty-ninth degree."

In *Twenty Thousand Leagues under the Sea* (1866), Verne describes a super-submarine whose aquanauts roam about underwater for months at a time. Only in recent years has technology been refined enough to give nuclear subs the capability of prolonged spells beneath the surface. Verne also predicted climate control, solar energy at home and at work, the pocket electrocardiograph and arsenals of weapons that could wipe out cities at the press of a button.

Keeping up with the Future

Today, as technology's complexities multiply, it takes a brave soul to be a predictor. The lone visionaries of the past had the leisure to flex their imaginations; they *knew* they were ahead of their time. But the predictors of the eighties can never be sure. First, they must struggle to assimilate the mass of scientific information. Then, they must strive to make themselves heard over the din of electronic communications. And even when they *are* heard, there's a very good chance they'll be proven wrong, if only because modern technology, that erratic beast, moves much faster or slower than expected. In a matter of a few years, fools and liars are made of the most astute forecasters.

In 1824, Margaret Fuller predicted the United States would be strung with railroad and telegraph lines from coast to coast. At the time there were only twenty miles of railroad track in the entire country, and the only way to travel from New York to San Francisco was around Cape Horn. It took ninety years for Margaret Fuller's vision to come true, but technology has since accelerated so rapidly that her grand-nephew, Buckminster Fuller, admits it's impossible to try forecasting our progress by the end of the century. A new age of helplessness — or humility — seems to have dawned for the prophets of science. In March, 1966, in a lecture on the year 2000 at San José State College in California, Fuller said:

> I am confident that I cannot predict for the year 2000. Though it is only a little over a generation forward, I do not believe that any human being can foresee with any accuracy as far ahead as . . . 35 years. What will go on in this next period will be more of a change than has occurred in the whole history of man on the whole earth.

Fuller's attempt to predict a mere ten years ahead served only to illustrate his point. At the time, he forecast the end of family motoring:

> We get onto a freeway . . . running in lines in opposite directions at 65 miles an hour, only five feet apart, with everybody practicing steering. A decade from now this will look rather silly . . . we will finish with our great highway programs just in time to turn them into some kind of roller-skating rink.

The oil crisis and the continuing pressure to ban cars from city centers show that Fuller's instincts were right. Nevertheless, he was — and still is — years ahead of his time. His prediction that industrialization will embrace the globe by 1985 is also likely to miss the mark, probably by at least ten years.

The Wright Brothers were mighty aviators but paltry predictors. Before Orville Wright flew into history by making the first manned flight from Kitty Hawk, North Carolina in 1903, neither brother had imagined man would fly so soon. In 1908, Wilbur Wright said, "I confess that in 1901 I said to my brother Orville that man would not fly for fifty years. Ever since I have distrusted myself and avoided all predictions . . ."

We are still waiting to see whether the inventor of the geodesic dome will be vindicated in his prediction of huge, tetrahedron-shaped floating cities. In *Utopia or Oblivion* (1969), Fuller described each city having living space for 30,000 families as well as room for industry and parkland. His man-made islands (each side would be roughly two miles long) would be moored offshore or strung across the ocean. He also envisaged giant, energy-saving domes covering downtown areas. His New York dome would measure two miles in diameter:

> . . . the dome calculated for mid-Manhattan has a surface which is only 1/85 the total area of the buildings which it would cover. It would reduce the energy losses either in winter heating or summer cooling to 1/85 the present energy cost, obviating snow removal. The cost saving in ten years would pay for the dome.

Like Fuller, writer and space consultant Arthur C. Clarke casts doubt on his own ability to predict. In *Profiles of the Future* (1958), he states:

> I will not have succeeded in looking very far ahead; for the one fact about the future of which we can be certain is that it will be utterly fantastic.

Yet Clarke hasn't been without his successes. In 1945, when he was a radar operator with the Royal Air Force, he came up with the idea of "synchronous orbit" communication satellites. Three decades later this proposal became reality. In 1947, he forecast the first rocket landing on the moon in 1959. As if in accordance with his wishes, the Russians' Lunar II touched down on September 13, 1959. And in 1958 he predicted a manned spacecraft would land in 1970. He was only one year off. The Apollo 11 astronauts stepped onto the lunar landscape on July 20, 1969.

Clarke, who has been called the "founder of the space age," maintains that the impact of communication satellites will equal or surpass that of the telephone in Europe and North America. Life in Third World nations will be revolutionized; only a single antenna will be required in each village to receive microwave broadcasts. In *Profiles of the Future*, he describes how satellites will be linked with giant information storehouses:

> The time will come when half the world's business will be transacted through vast memory banks beneath the Arizona

desert, the Labrador muskeg, the Mongolian steppes, or wherever land is cheap and useless for any other purpose.

Clarke also sees the day when surgery by satellite will be commonplace. Imagine, for instance, that a patient in Jackson Hole, Wyoming needs a delicate operation and the nearest specialist is in San Francisco. By satellite, the surgeon could operate by manipulating remote-controlled robot arms similar to those used in laboratories and nuclear plants.

Trains and cargo ships, those draft horses of the Industrial Revolution, will be replaced by hovercraft and freighter submarines by

The world's first communication satellite is checked by American technicians before launching.

Back in 1819, the British government gave mathematician Charles Babbage a $40,000 grant to develop the world's first computer — perhaps the most far-sighted government move of all time. Babbage spent the rest of his life and resources trying to perfect an "analytical engine," but was foiled by the lack of precision engineering. His biographer later made the wry observation, "This extraordinary monument of theoretical genius accordingly remains, and doubtless will forever remain, a theoretical possibility."

1990, says Clarke. Traveling at an average speed of 150 miles per hour, large sea-going hovercraft could leave New York at six o'clock in the morning and be in London by nine in the evening. Cargo submarines, towing barges shaped like streamlined balloons, would save energy, since they're more efficient than surface ships.

Clarke also says private cars will become smaller, with an electric motor in each wheel, and will be guided on highways by computer. With the computer at the wheel, he reckons manual steering may well be against the law by 1995. Other developments foreseen by Clarke include sea and space mining, space colonies by 1990 and contact with extra-terrestrial creatures by the 2030s.

By 2300, suggests Isaac Asimov, New York's extremely prolific writer-scientist, waste will be our major raw material for both manufacturing and energy. Hydrogen will be used to recycle consumer wastes to generate energy. But our greatest source will be the sun, whose rays will be trapped by orbiting solar power stations. These stations will be maintained by self-sufficient space colonies spinning in orbit around the earth, each containing a population of about three-quarters of a million.

Russian-born Asimov, who has written at least 203 books and 1,000 newspaper and magazine articles, says the day will soon be here when we can make telephone purchases from stores twenty-four hours a day; we'll simply tune in to catalogues on our TV screens. At the same time, we'll have audio-visual communication links between the home and workplace. An accountant, for example, could get the figures he wanted at home by tinkering with the controls of his video-phone-TV-computer. This domestic technology would mean, among other things, that the knowledge of the world's libraries could be at the fingertips of anyone who wanted to push the right buttons.

The modern age poses extraordinary difficulties for Fuller, Clarke, Asimov and others extending the line that started with Roger Bacon in the thirteenth century. The greatest dilemma is that the very technology their forerunners helped bring to life now threatens to replace them. More and more, our society is veering toward computerized planning to prophesy what we must do, and how and when. Although we still have our prophets, the future of technological prediction appears to rest with the calculations of futurists and their research teams. Mass technology, naturally, breeds mass prediction. But we must have faith that there'll still be room for imagination, that the grand solo tradition will be perpetuated by science-fiction writers with the will to astonish us. For if there's a lesson to be learned from the history of technological prediction, it is this: we can't do without our imaginings.

Isaac Asimov, the living legend of science-fiction who calls himself "an aging child prodigy," is not the most optimistic of men. In March, 1979, after gazing into the crystal ball presented to him by *Omni* magazine to mark his 200th book, he declared, "Unless we control our population and find alternate energy sources, I think civilization will break down in the lifetime of those now living — in another thirty to fifty years."

George Orwell and the world of Big Brother.

9 Negative Utopias

"What will happen to us when the State takes down the
   the manor wall,
When there is no more private shooting or fishing,
   when the trees are all cut down,
When faces are all dials and cannot smile or frown . . ."

Louis MacNeice

Beast in our Future

Now that his boot is in the door, Big Brother will soon be watching
us. Society will degenerate into an over-organized mass of defeated
drones. We'll be enslaved by faceless manipulators; we'll fall victim
to the perversion of science. It matters little whether the State keeps
us smiling through conditioning and mind control as in Aldous
Huxley's *Brave New World*, or whether — scraping to survive shortages, duped by Doublethink and spied on by our neighbors as well
as the Thought Police — we're left trembling in the brute world of
George Orwell's *1984*. Either way, every quirk and insight that
makes us individuals will be mashed to acceptable pulp. State control
is the name of the game. Control of who we are, what we do and
how we feel.

With velvet glove or mail gauntlet, totalitarian subjection is our
future, according to many twentieth century philosopher-novelists.
None presents a bleaker prospect than George Orwell, who developed a strong social conscience while breaking through the suf-
focating environment of upper-middle-class English society. Disturbed by what he considered a worldwide trend toward totalitarianism,
he began identifying signs of the monster's awakening in England.
Ten years before the publication of *1984*, his masterpiece of social
prediction, Orwell wrote *Coming up for Air* (1939) in which the
English protagonist voices his fears:

> . . . all the things you've got in the back of your mind, the
> things you're terrified of, the things you tell yourself are just
> a nightmare or only happen in foreign countries. The bombs,
> the food queues, the rubber truncheons, the barbed wire, the

coloured shirts, the slogans, the enormous faces, the machine guns squirting out of bedroom windows. It's all going to happen . . . it's just something that's got to happen.

In *1984* it happens with a vengeance. The world is divided into the superpowers of Oceania, Eurasia and Eastasia, dreadful places where the populations ceaselessly endure a "warfare of limited aims" waged to boost production rather than make territorial gains. The novel is set in England (part of Oceania) where society has deteriorated into a hell of rotting accommodation, food and power shortages and interminable bureaucracy, where history is rewritten, truth distorted and where the cellars of the Ministry of Love are the cradle of torture and execution. The whole shambles is overseen by Big Brother, the dictatorial symbol of the State that subdues its citizens by watching them on "telescreens" installed in every dwelling and workplace. The hero, Winston Smith, holds out as long as he can against the regime but, through torture and manipulation, his resistance is broken down and twisted into affection for his oppressors. By the end of the book, he loves Big Brother.

An automobile graveyard.

Utopia Goes Sour

But long before Winston Smith rebelled in vain, philosophers were questioning man's collective future. Hoping for the best, they proposed happy societies called "utopias," from the Greek meaning "no place." These "no places" have always been with us, located just around the next bend in time.

Plato drew up the first utopia around 370 B.C. His *Republic* is a well-reasoned dialogue about a perfect society where wives and children are held in common, where men and women enjoy equal educational opportunities and share all pursuits, warlike or peaceful. Even as Plato stressed that power "must be confined to men who are not in love with it," he foresaw his warning would go unheeded. He knew the dangerous pendulum effect of too much openness in society:

> . . . the only outcome of too much freedom is likely to be excessive subjection in the State or in the individual; which means that the culmination of liberty in democracy is precisely what prepares the way for the cruelest extreme of servitude under a despot.

A map of More's *Utopia*, back in the days before utopias turned into dictatorships.

In the centuries that followed, Plato's warning was forgotten. By the time Sir Thomas More's *Utopia* appeared in 1516, any skepticism about social progress had long since evaporated. More's land of fable featured work for all and a national system of education promoting the sacrifice of individual desires to the common good. Hope continued to flourish with Sir Francis Bacon's *New Atlantis* (1627), an imaginary island community inspired by emerging scientific progress where everyone assumes knowledge and science will improve the quality of life.

The first attempt to forecast what life would be like in the twentieth century was made in 1763 by the anonymous author of *The Reign of George VI, 1900-1925*. He was right about one thing — George VI did sit on the English throne in this century — but the writer did little more than project a perfected version of the civilization he knew. He wasn't much of a predictor. His twentieth century shows no increase in population; cities remain small and science and technology haven't begun to change people's lifestyles. In 1770, a book called *The Year 2440* by Sebastian Mercier maintained the optimistic tradition by describing a world of peace and harmony. Slavery has been eliminated, Latin and Greek are no longer taught in the schools, marriage dowries have been abolished and people are so hospitable that inns have disappeared out of sheer neglect! Again, the rapid and all-embracing changes wrought by science were not anticipated.

It was in 1793 that the most accurate of the optimists, the Marquis de Condorcet, published a work grandly entitled *Sketch for an Historical Picture of the Progess of the Human Mind*. The Frenchman, too, predicted slavery would disappear — but he went much further. He foresaw great strides in science and social welfare, the spread of birth control, the political independence of the New World colonies and improvements in farming that would produce more and better food from the same acreage. But as the regimentation of the Industrial Revolution took hold, cracks began to appear in the foundations of hope.

While divining many of the more attractive aspects of future society, Bulwer Lytton glimpsed the effects of technological over-development. In *The Coming Race* (1871), Lytton describes an advanced people called the *Vril-ya* who enjoy peace and equality, free education and generous allotments of leisure time. Poverty is abolished, because the rich ensure the upkeep of the destitute, and society has the services of robots, television, flying machines and sleep-teaching devices. Yet for all their good fortune, the people aren't happy. Literature has disappeared, music has become thoroughly mechanical, history has been eliminated and the *Vril-ya*, weary of having so much, so easily, have begun to decline. All that flourishes is science which, as Lytton says, is devoted to "social conservation and the comforts of . . . daily life." In his own way, Lytton is the first to sound a warning bell for unborn generations.

No work by a social predictor has been able to match the instant acclaim of Edward Bellamy's *Looking Backward 2000-1887*. Within fourteen months of its publication in 1888, the book had racked up sales of a quarter million in the United States alone. Set in Boston in the year 2000, the book is founded on the naive premise that state socialism would lead to the best of all possible worlds. The hero awakens from a hypnotic trance to find the city magnificently transformed. Everywhere are superb examples of modern architecture and beautiful parks. The anxieties, squalor, crime and greed of the past have given way to a classless society where private property is no more and no one works past the age of forty-five. Bellamy's idealism leads him to an image of socialism and science marching shoulder-to-shoulder toward a glorious future. "The State," he writes, "had at length become the one capitalist . . . the sole employer."

While Bellamy was predicting a life of bounty and brotherhood, William Morris, who reviewed the book in 1899, perceived the misery and despotism lurking behind the serried ranks of happy factory faces. ". . . although he *tells* us," wrote Morris, "that work is no burden to anyone, the impression which he produces is that of a huge standing army, tightly-drilled, compelled by some mysterious fate to unceasing anxiety for the production of wares to satisfy every caprice, however wasteful and absurd."

Yet William Morris' refusal to be swayed by Bellamy's utopia was mild indeed compared with the very first totalitarian novel: Jack London's *The Iron Heel* (1907). There was more to London than adventure stories. His book forecasts a ruthless North American dictatorship enforced by secret police, concentration camps and a muzzled Press. London was far ahead of his time in foretelling the cruelly repressive regimes that were to rule Russia, Germany and Italy. As the dust jacket copy on modern editions of the book proclaims, *The Iron Heel* was written when "Mussolini was a democratic agitator, Lenin and Stalin obscure conspirators and Hitler an unsuccessful artist." London's achievement lay in breaking out of the mold of optimism that had shaped all socially predictive literature until that time.

London's terrifying vision was confirmed by Eugene Zamiatin, a little known Russian author whose novel *We* was written just three years after the Russian Revolution of 1917. The death of hope brought on by World War One is dramatically evident in this work. Zamiatin's future is dominated by a one-state world (called, ironically, the United State) which offers stability, perfection and happiness to a population with numbers for names. But the calm is broken by the narrator called D-503 who discovers the life-giving forces of chaos, passion and rebellion. The State crushes the uprising by performing lobotomies on every individual, the narrator included, thereby ensuring them a lifetime of peaceful obedience. The narrator's final submissive message is: "Reason must prevail."

> "Modern industry will tear away from the family the sentimental veil and reduce it to a mere money relation." — Karl Marx

1984

But no predicted rule by cudgel has caught the public imagination like George Orwell's *1984*. For years, Orwell's future has cropped up in discussion about the way society is evolving. Today, both the year itself and the realization of the book's message are close at hand. Although we have yet to be shackled by *1984*'s soulless system, it's frightening to consider that some 100 of the book's 137 social, political and scientific predictions have already come true. Many of these developments, seemingly perfected for humane and peaceful purposes, need only a substantial threat — war, perhaps, or revolution — to be used against the people they are now supposed to serve. Even if their purpose is not perverted, they are still designed to serve the government rather than the citizen. Dependence on the State is stressed while individual thought, self-determination and decision-making are discouraged.

Orwell foretold the break-up of the family unit (the American divorce rate more than doubled between 1963 and 1975) and wrote

Adolf Hitler, a source of inspiration for Orwell's *1984*.

of the decline and degradation of the English language into New-speak where words are chopped and joined and vocabulary is reduced, all to promote Doublethink. Governments love to mangle the language into slick, easy-to-understand blocks. Take "Lottario," for example, a word dreamed up by the government of the Canadian province of Ontario to describe its lottery which, in itself, is an example of another Orwell prediction fulfilled. In many ways, *1984* is here now. Here are a few of the socio-scientific breakthroughs that bear out Orwell's forecasts:

- Behavior modification, including lobotomy and "truth" drugs, through psychoscience. There's been a tenfold increase in American brain scientists since 1963; they now number more than 6,000. Psychoscience has accumulated more than 3,000 behavior-modifying therapies to outstrip the ghoulishness of Orwell's future. In 1975, it was revealed that brain researchers, funded by U.S. military intelligence, had been working on methods of hypnotic interrogation and behavior control through ultrasonics and electromagnetic radiation. Two years later, it was disclosed that the C.I.A. had spent $25 million over 17 years studying such behavior-altering drugs as L.S.D. and pentothal.
- Large telescreens for public viewing. A popular, harmless feature of many sports stadiums — but consider their potential to shape public opinion.
- Police helicopters. A symbol of strength, appearing on the side of Right in many a TV adventure story. Orwell realized they could be used to snoop on and control the population.
- Doublethink, which Orwell defined as "the power of holding two contradictory beliefs in one's mind simultaneously and accepting both of them." Today Doublethink is used almost unconsciously in political propaganda and in government, business and industrial public relations. In the late 60s the Nixon administration acted out Doublethink by covertly ordering telephone taps, sponsoring break-ins and opening mail while at the same time upholding domestic law and order and decrying civil disobedience.
- Security hardware. The remote heart beat sensor, the "tone-of-voice" analyzer, two-way televisions and sensitive omni-directional microphones have been standard equipment for police and intelligence organizations for some time. While the

Freedom is abolished in Harlan Ellison's *Silent in Gehenna* where universities, in the year 2012, are circled by electrified fences and overseen by armed robots.

A short story by Isaac Asimov called *All the Troubles of the World* predicts a future dominated by Multivac, a Washington-based computer that acts as a clearing house for every available fact about every individual.

The antiquated streetcars of Asunción, Paraguay are shabby, rickety and uneconomical. But they're kept running, so it's said, because of a prediction that the Paraguayan dictator, General Alfredo Stroessner, will lose power once they're replaced. Stroessner has ruled the nation since 1954.

scientists of Oceania were hard at work devising ways to find out what people were thinking, we've reached the stage where Thought Police technology is about to be made available to the public. Early in 1979, a New York company announced it would soon have a lie-detector wristwatch on the market selling for $29.95. A tiny silicon chip in the timepiece measures voice stress and informs its wearer whether the person being questioned is telling the truth. And in the summer of 1979, New York scientist Adam Reed was said to be on the verge of discovering the code in the human brain that will give others access to an individual's thoughts.

- Data banks for use in police surveillance and control. A report on police computers in Britain (*New Scientist*, January 18, 1979) brought to mind the sinister world of *1984* when it said, "The perspective which emerges is not of fast, fact-finding systems to enhance police efficiency but determinedly crafted mechanisms for official control." The computerized Criminal Names Index in Britain contains 3.8 million names of those convicted of allegedly "more serious offences," yet on this list are also those guilty of petty infringements such as wasting police time and offences under the Rent Acts. Not long ago, criminal names on file numbered 2.2 million, before the records were boosted with lesser offenders as names were transferred from Scotland Yard dossiers to the national computer. As a report of the British Data Protection Committee pointed out, "The linking of actual personal information about an identifiable individual with speculative data about criminal activity could pose a grave threat . . ."

How long, then, until privacy is gnawed away to this Orwellian extreme?

Always the eyes watching you and the voice enveloping you. Asleep or awake, working or eating, indoors or out of doors, in the bath or in bed — no escape. Nothing was your own except the few cubic centimetres inside your skull.

The *1984* individual, bombarded with misleading information, comes to doubt his own judgment and knowledge, even about the most straightforward facts:

In the end the Party would announce that two and two made five, and you would have to believe it . . . And what was terrifying was not that they would kill you for thinking otherwise, but that they might be right. For, after all, how do we know that two and two make four? Or that the force of gravity works? Or that the past is unchangeable?

In today's world, we have already reached the stage where much of the population relies on State-run lotteries for excitement. In *1984* the "proles," or masses, were similarly transfixed:

> It was probable that there were some millions of proles for whom the Lottery was the principal if not the only reason for remaining alive. It was their delight, their folly, their anodyne, their intellectual stimulant.

Orwell also describes the loss of effective literacy. No one writes letters any more; they simply select printed postcards and strike out the phrases that are inapplicable, a substitute that can be found in many of our offices, factories, schools and universities.

The Population Pacified

The "hunting down and destruction of books" spelled out in *1984* was adopted by Ray Bradbury as the central theme of his grimly futuristic American novel *Fahrenheit 451*. The title refers to the temperature at which book paper catches fire. The few remaining people who dare to read books live in fear of the "firemen" who, no longer needed for their traditional role since the advent of fire-proofing, are used to start fires instead. Again, book-burning is ordered by a shadowy totalitarian government that wants to minimize thinking and its revolutionary potential. Bradbury blames no one but the people themselves for their plight, pointing a finger at the "most dangerous enemy to truth and freedom, the solid unmoving cattle of the majority." After all, most people surrendered their rights by giving up reading even before the book ban was introduced. Explains Beatty, the malevolent fire chief:

> There was no dictum, no declaration, no censorship, to start with, no! Technology, mass exploitation and minority pressure carried the trick, Thank God. Today, thanks to them, you can stay happy all the time, you are allowed to read comics, the good old confessions, or trade journals.

Television, flashing and shimmering from giant screens that cover three or four walls of a living room, keeps the public in a state of

The Decline of the West, Oswald Spengler's masterpiece, says it all. A great believer in recurring trends, the German philosopher (1880-1936) maintained that Western civilization was sliding toward disintegration and final collapse. Spengler foresaw society after 2000 huddled in vast cities "laid out for ten to twenty million inhabitants, spread over enormous areas of countryside, with buildings that will dwarf the biggest of today's, and notions of traffic and communication that we should regard as fantastic to the point of madness."

Yesterday's vision is already today's reality. But we haven't yet suffered from the massive wars in which, said Spengler, "Continents will be staked, India, China, Africa, Russia, Islam called out, new technics and tactics played and counter played."

soggy servitude. They don't think, they don't criticize, they just watch one soap opera after another. Or they stick minute receivers in their ears and soak up the blare of transistor radios to escape the world around them. Real conversation has been phased out, a trend already apparent in our society where radio and television are replacing the spoken word. The kindergarten age is lowered year after year so children can be manipulated more easily, while intellectuals who refuse to give up thinking for themselves· are hounded: "... they say there's lots of old Harvard degrees on the tracks between here and Los Angeles. Most of them are wanted and hunted in the cities." Bradbury could be talking about life today when he describes, once more through fire chief Beatty, the prevailing lifestyle of the pacified generation:

> School is shortened, discipline relaxed, philosophies, histories, languages dropped, English and spelling gradually gradually neglected, finally almost completely ignored. Life is immediate, the job counts, pleasure lies all about after work. Why learn anything save pressing buttons, pulling switches, fitting nuts and bolts?

When Aldous Huxley wrote *Brave New World* in 1931 he set his sweetly manipulative dictatorship in the year 632 A.F. (After Ford, the father of mass production), thinking it would be at least another six hundred years before this sick order could possibly be established. Yet even as he wrote, the seeds of his smoothly regimented world were being planted in Germany and Russia, and by 1946 he was shocked into writing, in a foreword to his novel: "Today it seems quite possible that the horror may be upon us within a single century. That is, if we refrain from blowing ourselves to smithereens in the interval." And in 1958, striving to keep pace with the rapid onset of his nightmare, Huxley proclaimed in *Brave New World Revisited:*

> The prophecies made in 1931 are coming true much sooner than I thought they would. The blessed interval between too little order and the nightmare of too much has not begun and shows no sign of beginning ... The nightmare of total organization, which I had situated in the seventh century After Ford, has emerged from the safe, remote future and is now awaiting us, just around the corner.

Brave New World, in which ten world Controllers run the globe, is the last word in social conditioning. Rather than terrorizing its subjects into doing its will, the government, operating with greater skill and cunning than Big Brother, soothes them into acquiescence. The population is graded according to intellectual and physical capabilities, and each group is inculcated with appropriate likes and dislikes. The family structure has been dismantled and all babies flow from test tubes. Standardization and sterility is all:

> "Ninety-six identical twins working ninety-six identical machines!" The voice was almost tremulous with enthusiasm. "You really know where you are. For the first time in history."

Fornication, however, is encouraged, and the slogan "everyone belongs to everyone else" is trotted out for mass adoption. Whereas enforced chastity helps induce the pent-up aggression desired by the State bosses in *1984*, the rulers of Huxley's world want a tranquilized, contented population to pay unquestioning homage to its leaders. And after a Nine Years' War, the masses are all too willing

With social disorder threatening, Huxley believed, people would gladly turn to a dictatorship for security.

Montreal psychiatrist Dr. Heinz Lehmann predicts that sedatives such as Valium will be used as commonly as aspirin within ten or fifteen years.

Dr. Lehmann, the man who introduced to North America the use of tranquilizing drugs to treat the mentally ill, is on record as saying, "We simply can't live without tranquilizers just as we cannot live without cars."

He also foresees the time when people who need a weekend away from it all will make a reservation at a mental hospital rather than a pleasure resort.

Such a weekend, he maintains, would not only provide freedom from the unceasing demands of business and society. It would also grant a unique opportunity for "guests" to snap at people to rid themselves of tension and not be snapped back at. "The grouchier a person became," says Lehmann, "the more gentle and understanding would be the treatment received from others."

to trade in their freedom for peace. To gently aid and enforce the conditioning process, there are institutions such as the College of Emotional Engineering and the Bureau of Propaganda. And the drug *soma* is issued to smooth away any remaining resentments or difficulties. The London-based Controller explains the success of this bondage without tears:

> The world's stable now. People are happy; they get what they want, and they never want what they can't get. They're well-off, they're safe; they're never ill; they're not afraid of death; they're blissfully ignorant of passion and old age . . . And if anything goes wrong, there's *soma*.

Huxley, the third son of a Victorian gentleman, tells in *Brave New World Revisited* how modern society will find it hard to resist totalitarian encroachment because so many people are "not on the spot"; they're occupied instead by "irrelevant other worlds of sport and soap opera, of mythology and metaphysical fantasy." Drugs, as we know, have become part of life in many societies, and increasing discussion about the possibility of legalizing possession of "soft" drugs such as marijuana brings Huxley's vision ever closer. As for tranquilizers, each year millions of prescriptions for Valium alone are filled out in the United States, not to mention other pill-popping Western nations. The conveyor belt thinking of Huxley's "sleep teaching" could be drummed into today's youngsters by a manipulative government; the technology has long been available. And although we're not yet producing the kind of test tube babies Huxley envisaged, the scientific world is rife with talk of cloning, while artificial insemination has produced bouncing offspring to the much-publicized delight of couples who feared they'd never experience the joys of parenthood.

In *Brave New World Revisited,* Huxley delivers a final prediction outlining the insidious way we'll lose our freedom. Only when it's too late will we realize how we've been deceived — stealthily and with subtlety, because we said "yes" when we should have said "no":

> . . . by ever more effective methods of mind-manipulation, the democracies will change their nature; the quaint old forms — elections, parliaments, Supreme Courts and all the rest — will remain . . . Democracy and freedom will be the theme of every broadcast and editorial — but democracy and freedom in a strictly Pickwickian sense. Meanwhile the ruling oligarchy

and its highly trained elite of soldiers, policemen, thought-manufacturers and mind-manipulators will quietly run the show as they see fit.

Vigilance or Oblivion

The classics of Orwell, Bradbury and Huxley have spawned countless novels and short stories based on the premise that society, beset by insoluble problems, is hurtling toward self-destruction. The anticipated doom of our cities and nations has become big business, with authors competing to present the most miserable outcome of all. But behind many of these commercial efforts is a real cry for help.

In Harry Harrison's *Make Room! Make Room!* (1966), overpopulation is the evil that pushes a desperate society down Disintegration Alley. New York is bulging with 35 million souls in the insufferably hot summer of 1999. Crime and inflation are rampant, food and water are scarce and even the sellers of weedcrumbs — "the cheapest and most tasteless nourishment ever consumed by man" — are attacked by starving crowds. Squatters huddle in the skeletons of old buildings or seek shelter in "villages" of old cars in disused parking lots. How will all this come about? Harry Harrison answers in the words of one of his characters:

> So mankind gobbled in a century all the world's resources that had taken millions of years to store up, and no one on the top gave a damn or listened to all the voices that were trying to warn them, they just let us overproduce and overconsume until now the oil is gone, the topsoil depleted and washed away, the trees chopped down, the animals extinct, the earth poisoned, and all we have to show for this is seven billion people fighting over the scraps that are left, living a miserable existence — and still breeding without control.

With the death of hope, the image of the boot prevails:

> We shall be robbed of our few remaining liberties; the Iron Heel will walk upon our faces.

So wrote Jack London in 1907. Orwell, in 1949, said the same thing when he put these words into the mouth of an accomplice of Big Brother:

> If you want a picture of the future, imagine a boot stamping on a human face — forever.

At the turn of the century, America will be a wasteland inhabited by racists who will hunt each other down with rifles, according to Alan Seymour in his novel *The Coming Self-Destruction of the United States of America* (1969).

Robert Silverberg scrapes the barrel of pessimism by showing us the aftermath of global nuclear destruction in a short story called *The Wind and the Rain*. A reclamation team has descended to Earth from a space colony settled by humans years before the annihilation. The narrator, a member of the clean-up squad, describes what he sees: "Toward the end here they all wore breathing suits, similar to ours but even more comprehensive. We find these suits lying around everywhere like the discarded shells of giant insects."

"They just let us overproduce and overconsume until now the oil is gone . . ." Harry Harrison in *Make Room! Make Room!*

Social philosopher Erich Fromm wrote in 1961 that "Orwell, like the authors of other negative utopias, is not a prophet of disaster. He wants to warn and to awaken us." More than simply forecasting, the social predictors are trying to shake us out of our lassitude. Their collective outlook doesn't *have* to be ours. They've seen the way we're going and they've eloquently voiced their warnings about the hazards that await us. But as predictable as our journey may seem, the destination is never fixed so long as we command the power of choice.

The boot may be jammed in the door of the future, but only because we've let it stay there — through apathy, through indifference or through ignorance of how savage and pitiless totalitarianism can be. We haven't *chosen* to be rid of it. Yet only by choosing can we maintain our freedom of choice. In choice lies our salvation. How we choose is how we predict our own future.

Earthrise, as seen by the Apollo 10 astronauts on the Moon's surface.

10 The Futurists

"Things do not happen — they are made to happen."

John F. Kennedy

Future, Inc.

Prediction has become big business in the last half of the twentieth century. The captains of this industry are the *futurists*, predictors whose methods differ radically from their counterparts in the rest of this book. The futurist is the predictor as technocrat, the predictor as scientist, the predictor who subordinates his ideas, instincts and imaginings to deduction and calculation. He hazards his predictions only after sorting through what German futurist Robert Jungk calls "the ever-increasing stream of fresh data informing man not only about the present state of the world, but also about the impact of his actions."

Government and industry hire futurists to chart the shape of tomorrow for the sake of progress, prosperity and, in the case of nuclear weaponry and depleting resources, for the sake of survival. They're highly-paid professionals with few metaphysical aspirations; most of them are prophets of profit. More than mere fancy or fascination, the future is their vocation. The future is where they live.

In spite of their practical persuasion, the futurists are really no less fantastic in their predicting than anyone else. It's as if they've paid special heed to French poet René Crevel who affirmed "No daring is fatal." Their boldness is rooted in faith and knowledge — faith in man's voracity for exploration and achievement and knowledge that we already possess the technology to realize what only thirty years ago would have been labeled impossible. Excepting fears of nuclear catastrophe, their predictions are generally optimistic, brimming with enthusiasm for man's ability to cope with difficulties on earth. And they're just as confident that he'll explore the heavens and inaugurate the era of space colonization.

It's this optimism that sets the futurists even further apart from the other predictors. Their hope contrasts radically with the stance of many prophets, from Nostradamus to the most obscure of present-day psychics, who are seduced by a future of chaos and destruction. But then, the futurists are obliged to be optimistic. They must have confidence in their own ability to anticipate and control the future; otherwise, to put it plainly, they'd be out of work. Theirs is the positive voice, the voice of reason in a clamorous world that often appears to be careening toward self-destruction.

The stamp of technological capability is printed on practically every prediction made by the futurists — and what could be more normal, since they're a product of the age that's compelled prediction to shed its amateur status? Although the practice of retaining professional predictors wasn't generally adopted until the early six-

What would become of the futurists without the ubiquitous computer? This machine has been pressed into doing duty as a prophet.

ties, the largest of the futurist concerns, the California-based Rand Corporation, was founded just after World War Two. Next came the Hudson Institute — the world-famous think tank run by Herman Kahn — that was set up near New York in 1961. Once these installations were operating, professional forums were founded between 1965 and 1970 where futurists could meet and swap ideas. Among the most notable are the International Futuribles Association (Paris, 1965), the World Future Society (Washington, 1966) and the Club of Rome (1968). Today, few corporative enterprises can afford not to employ or contract futurists to sit in the crow's nest and scan the horizons of their endeavors.

The Rand Corporation, which earned more than $48 million in 1978, makes predictions for anyone who will pay for them. Although its initial objective was to draw up military projections, the corporation has since extended its expertise to include civil matters such as medical care, housing supply and geothermal energy development. A Rand report, written in the early 70s, pointed to the feasibility of towing icebergs north from Antarctica to relieve parched tracts of California. Saudi Arabia, desperate for potable water, latched onto this proposal and was actively considering an $80 million project to tow a 100 million ton iceberg 5,000 miles to the Red Sea. The iceberg would be swathed in plastic foam and pulled by five tugs at a speed of one nautical mile an hour. This scheme is surely as fanciful as anything the ancient predictors could have imagined.

George Washington (1732-1799) became a canal promoter because he foresaw the probability of the U.S. Civil War one hundred years before it happened. Though a slave owner himself, he felt sure economic and social disaster lay ahead for America unless slavery was abolished. To prevent this catastrophe, he believed the South's economic dependence on slavery would have to be ended through rapid industrialization. The swiftest, most effective method was to build a canal linking the new factories in Virginia with the sea. Before becoming a general and the first president of the United States, Washington was the head of a company formed to carry out this mission.

"A Slightly Optimistic" View

The futurists who make the most probing predictions are those who assume responsibility for weighing the prospects of mankind and planet Earth over the next few decades. Herman Kahn and Alvin Toffler, the kingpins of modern futurism, both feel conditions will get worse before they get better, but they *will* get better. The Hudson Institute, directed by Kahn, is retained by most major governments in the Western world, as well as by more than fifty multi-national corporations. The Institute produces scenarios on subjects ranging from defence to social medicine, from agriculture to politics. Armed with fifty professional staff members and one hundred consultants, its avowed aim is to provide projections of such comprehensiveness that the real future, when it arrives, will be "surprise-free."

In *A World Turning Point and a Better Prospect for the Future* (1975), Kahn and his associate, William H. Brown, predict:

- A gradual decline in the world birthrate leading to a generally affluent world by 2100.
- A clean environment for Western nations by 1985.
- A lessening of severe food shortages.
- The solution of the energy crisis by 1995 through technical conservation, lifestyle adjustments and the concerted development of new energy sources. By 2100, a variety of inexpensive alternatives to fossil fuels will be widely available.
- The continuing availability of metal ores, especially iron and aluminum, which are so abundant as to be practically inexhaustible.

Predictor for hire: one of the stars of the future business, Herman Kahn of the Hudson Institute.

Hopeful as this forecast may be, Kahn, a cheery 300-pound cherub of a man, has since said that "things will get very shaky towards the end of the century." He warns of the ever-present dangers of nuclear war and nuclear terrorism and says aerosol emissions and the burning of fossil fuels threaten the earth's atmosphere. In the Hudson Institute report *A Slightly Optimistic World Context for 1975-2000* (1974), Kahn predicts a dramatic rise in the world's standard of living. Barring the outbreak of nuclear war, he expects Japan to become one of the world's leading nations with an economy superior to Russia's and China's. These nations, Kahn believes, will remain hostile to the West. In America, he foresees urban sprawl creating megalopolises that will embrace half the population. The three largest will be *Boswash, Chipitts* and *Sansan. Boswash* will gobble up every city between Boston and Washington, *Chipitts* will join Chicago and Pittsburgh and include Cleveland, Buffalo, Detroit, Akron and Rochester, while *Sansan* will stretch all the way from San Diego to San Francisco.

By the year 2000, the Hudson Institute projects there will be a national data center in the United States where records will be kept on each and every citizen. And Kahn anticipates the invention of a computer intelligent enough to rival man. In an interview broadcast on the Canadian national radio network (CBC) on June 6, 1979, he said:

> Nobody has ever written a careful, rigorous statement as to why a computer could not duplicate, or even surpass, human beings. And maybe by the end of the century they *will* be surpassing human beings . . . That will change man's attitude toward man.

Alvin Toffler maintains there is "no such thing as prediction in any absolute sense. The best forecast should be taken with more than the usual grain of doubt." This might be construed as Toffler's way of preparing a safety net in case he's failed by the most precipitous of his predictions. Though he zealously qualifies his optimism, he is, at least, optimistic. At a World Future Society press conference in June, 1975, the author of *Future Shock*, which racked up sales of over six million, predicted painful progress toward a better life for all:

> The years immediately ahead will no doubt be painful. But if the notion of automatic "progress" is naive, so is the notion

Dumping of oil, chemicals and sewage will kill our oceans, predicts British science-fiction writer, Brian Aldis. Already, the increasing incidence of oil spills is confirming the worst fears of environmentalists. "With dead oceans, the rest of the world will die," Aldis bluntly states.

of inevitable "retrogression." If we can look beyond the immediate, we glimpse breakthroughs to something not merely new, but in many ways better and more just. To quote Raymond Fletcher [a British member of Parliament] . . . "All these alarming symptoms that so frighten us — they may be birth symptoms instead of death symptoms."

New ways of travel on this planet are high on the futurists' list of priorities.

In *Future Shock* (1971), Toffler proclaims our entry into the "super-industrial revolution," a transformation that owes much to the astuteness of multi-national corporations that use futurists to

ensure profitable expansion. In *The Eco-Spasm Report* (1975), Toffler argues that this revolution is no less than "the breakdown of industrial civilization on the planet and the first fragmentary appearance of a wholly new and dramatically different social order; a super-industrial civilization that will be technological but no longer industrial." Talk about self-fulfilling prophecy! Often the futurists' projections have created fast developing new industries with their subsequent sub-industries. For example, micro-circuitry, initially developed for military purposes, gave birth to the multi-billion dollar mini-computer boom.

The trouble is, says Toffler, that while the multi-nationals are gearing up for the future, the politicians are not. They habitually think in four-year cycles, whereas the future demands long-term solutions. To sell the public on a national plan for the next twenty-five to fifty years is politically impossible . . . and therein lies a major source of crisis for the years ahead. What's more, Toffler assures us we'll be in even deeper trouble unless we ensure citizen involvement in politics at all levels of government. In an address to the U.S. Committee on Anticipatory Democracy on September 11, 1975, he declared:

> Under conditions of high speed change, a democracy without the ability to anticipate condemns itself to death. But an anticipatory government without effective citizen participation and, indeed, control may be no less lethal. The future must neither be ignored nor captured by an elite. Only anticipatory democracy can provide a way out of the contradiction in which we find ourselves.

Space and Energy

Gerard O'Neill has little patience with such brooding analysis. Stress and strain, doubt and fear, don't figure in his ambitious designs. "Problems? Humbug!" he snorts while selling us a future in space with all the fervor of a Bible-thumping evangelist. O'Neill, a Princeton University professor specializing in particle physics, seems to be unaware of the space cut-backs in these times of austerity. He says if only the Western world would set aside its preoccupations with economic woes and mount a full-blooded space program, the first colony could be orbiting the earth as early as 1990. At the second General Assembly of the World Future Society on July 23, 1975, he summed up his mighty vision with these words:

". . . it is more probable than not that in fifty years' time men may be less secure, less well fed, and clothed and housed less comfortably than they are today, and that in that retrogressive age it may already have become as difficult and dangerous to travel from San Francisco to London or Paris as it was to go from London to Moscow in the thirteenth century." (From an October 1931 magazine article by H.G. Wells titled "What will this World be like Fifty Years from now?")

The energy crisis will force Canadian holidaymakers to spend their winter breaks at resort hotels in Canada offering tropical conditions simulated indoors, predicts Richard Crosby, president of Toronto's Creative Research Group.

The human race stands now on the threshold of a new frontier whose richness is a thousand times greater than that of the new Western World of 500 years ago.

O'Neill maintains the surface of a planet is "not a very good place to house a post-industrial society." Instead, he'd locate his first colony at "L-5," a point in space roughly half-way from the earth to the moon. The moon would yield ninety-eight per cent of all materials necessary to the colony's construction, which would start with a hunk of metal ferried out by space shuttle. The pioneering community would have a population of 2,000 workmen, while a supplementary group of 200 would establish a moon base to mine the ores for the colony's expansion. In time, satellite power stations would be built to beam solar power to earth for integration into the electric grid. This way, the space community would repay the heavy initial capital investment.

Island I — a colony composed of only workers — is relatively small and shaped like a hollow metal doughnut. Model I, his first complete space community, has room for 10,000 people and is composed of two cylinders, each 3,280 feet long and 328 feet wide (about three times the length but the same weight as a giant super-tanker). Model II would also be cylindrical, but its internal area would be three times as large, big enough to shelter 100,000 people. Model III would be larger still and its residents would mine asteroids instead of the moon for essential metals. Model IV offers dual cylinders lengthened to nineteen and widened to four miles! Several million people would live there. The colony would produce its own internal weather system and would be large enough to encompass an 8,000 foot mountain range. In fact, most of O'Neill's colonies would have forests, lakes, rivers, mountains and even clouds. Outside mirrors would simulate the movement of the sun across the sky as seen from Earth. Eventually, O'Neill envisages space residents settling in spheres measuring twelve miles in diameter. He speculates:

> By 2150, there could be more people living in space than on earth . . . Earth might serve mainly as a tourist attraction — a carefully-preserved monument to man's origin.

O'Neill's blueprint for the future has proved so popular that enthusiasts in the United States have started a club that produces a monthly bulletin called *L-5 News*. O'Neill commented on this de-

velopment with characteristic enthusiasm: ". . . in terms of public response," he said, "space colonization may be a phenomenon at least as powerful as the environmental movement."

Freeman Dyson, O'Neill's mentor and another Princeton physicist, sees space colonization shaping up in the asteroid belt that lies beyond the moon. In 1970, Dyson, along with scientist Ted Taylor, proposed Project Orion, a scheme to launch a space probe the size of a small city by detonating thermo-nuclear bombs behind a "pusher plate" attached to the back of the vehicle. When this project was attacked by various "ban-the-bomb" groups, Dyson and Taylor

Space colonization is a favored alternative to the earth's crowded surface. Here is an artist's conception of Skylab.

turned to lasers as a way to propel and guide the probe from earth, thereby eliminating the multi-bomb engine.

Dyson — who compared the relative costs of the Pilgrim Fathers who made the *Mayflower* voyage to America in 1620 with the projected price of space pioneering and found they tallied at $40,000 a head — says we will make big commitments to space over the next ten years if only because space technology shows all the signs of generating vast amounts of revenue. As Richard Hiscocks, vice-president of the Canadian National Research Council, said in 1976, "We have learned that the spur of industrial progress is in the marketplace, not simply in developing new technology . . . In the communications/information area alone, sixty-seven different services/products could be originated in orbit, a small indication of the enormous potential in this one area."

Jesco von Puttkamer, program director of NASA's Long Range Study Group, predicts man will be manufacturing in space within the next few decades from necessity rather than choice. He believes soaring world population and consumption together with dwindling raw materials, energy and habitable land will force nations into space; the only alternative would be constant war. In the June, 1979 *Futurist* he says:

Three Mile Island — just a preliminary to "the greatest catastrophe in the world?"

The commercialization of space, because it will allow continued world economic growth, will be instrumental in making space colonization tenable, supportable, and practical.

Space can be used most productively over the next few years to generate energy with the help of solar satellites, says von Puttkamer. But Glenn T. Seaborg, one of the "midwives" of the first atomic bomb and co-discoverer of plutonium, is convinced future energy needs can only be met through nuclear resources and, perhaps, coal. Seaborg, a Nobel Prize winner, has spent much of his life vigorously defending nuclear power against environmentalists who believe we are dicing with death in pursuing the nuclear option. "No technology has been born and developed with the regard for human safety and well-being that is inherent in the development of nuclear energy," he declares. In *Man and Atom* (1971), written in collaboration with William R. Corliss, he argues that we are fast approaching a series of crises. But like all futurists, he believes we're on the verge of a breakthrough:

> Nuclear energy holds one key — a crucial one — to the successful resolution of these crises . . . not only will we be able to raise a great part of the world's people to a decent standard of living, but we will be able to move all mankind ahead into a new era of human advancement — human advancement which takes place in harmony with the natural environment that must support it.

Yet since the nuclear mishap at Three Mile Island in March, 1979, the world hasn't been so eager to accept this verdict. According to another Nobel Prize winner, physicist Dr. Linus Pauling, there's scant reason for optimism. He maintains that if something else doesn't trigger "the greatest catastrophe in the world," our nuclear experimenting will. Pauling's introduction to *Nuclear Power: The Unviable Option* (1976) by John J. Berger contains one of the most doom-laden predictions to be found anywhere:

> I am afraid that within twenty-five or fifty years there will occur the greatest catastrophe in the history of the world. It might well result from a world war, which could destroy civilization and might be the end of the human race; or civilization might be destroyed and the human race brought to an end because of the collapse of the natural systems upon which it depends. The end of civilization might result from changes in the weather

Politics are often responsible for prediction confliction. These two predictions of Canadian oil reserves could hardly be further apart:

Canada's total petroleum reserves represent 923 years' supply for natural gas and 392 years for oil. The tough job is getting sales.

Canada's energy minister Joe Greene in a 1971 petroleum sales pitch to U.S. buyers

The outlook for the Canadian oil industry is not favorable. With the possible exception of the Bent Horn discovery in the Arctic islands, there has not been a major oil discovery in Canada since 1965, and crude oil reserves are declining rapidly.

W.G. Lugg, policy specialist for the Canadian Department of Energy in his 1976 report in the Canada Minerals Yearbook

Eighty-six year old Arnold Toynbee, the British philosopher-historian, said just before his death in 1975, "I believe the human race will not commit suicide — it will stop just short of that."

As early as 1895, H.G. Wells forecast the brinkmanship of guerilla movements in modern society. The theft of a deadly virus and subsequent ransom demands in his story *The Stolen Bacillus* presages former Ugandan dictator Idi Amin's plot to steal atomic bombs, hide them in his embassies around the world and blackmail Western nations.

induced by governments to improve the yield of crops, or might end by the rapid destruction of ozone layers in the stratosphere, or by the accumulation of poisonous wastes that would make the air unbreathable and water undrinkable.

Another possibility is that the construction of more and more electric power plants depending on nuclear fission would lead to a catastrophe. The plan now is to construct immense nuclear power plants by the hundreds. I believe that no more nuclear fission power plants should be constructed.

Without a doubt, nuclear war and disastrous mismanagement of our nuclear resources is what futurists fear most. While none are willing to predict an all-out nuclear holocaust, the topic thrums persistently in their reckonings. Recently Rand Corporation staff produced a report on the possible use of nuclear weapons by terrorists. And Israeli political scientist Yehezkel Dror has advanced the possibility of "insane" nations delivering nuclear ultimatums and minority groups obtaining the formula for disaster and holding governments to ransom. He suggests we might see newspaper headlines like these:

SOUTH AFRICA USES NUCLEAR THREATS
    TO SAVE WHITES
STUDENT ANARCHISTS ADOPT
    COUNTER-POPULATION TERROR

If the European futurists of the Club of Rome opt for pessimism, it's not because they especially fear the nuclear threat. *Everything* seems to be getting them down. A book based on their findings called *The Limits to Growth* (1972) makes depressing reading. Here's a sample:

> If the present growth trends in world population, industrialization, pollution, food production, and resources depletion continue unchanged, the limits of growth on this planet will be reached some time within the next one hundred years. The most probable result will be a rather sudden and uncontrollable decline in both population and industrial capacity.

But for *every* gloomy prediction there's a futurist with a buoyant rebuttal. Enter F.M. Esfandiary who declares, "Limits to growth? What limits? There are NO limits to growth. The only limits are in some people's imagination and vision." (*Futurist*, June, 1978). This

Iranian-born writer, philosopher, designer and planner sees man evolving into a super-species immune to aging and death. Esfandiary forecasts that by the year 2000, average life expectancy will be over 100 years; human immortality will be but a few years away. He envisages the introduction of durable, artificial eyes, ears, heart, lungs, kidney and other vital organs and believes the progressive increase in mechanical/electrical transplants will lead at last to the bionic man. Accompanying modifications to the body will be a change in our attitude toward Earth. We'll leave behind our "earth-icity," our planetary provincialism, to make a home in space. Esfandiary sees people moving restlessly in floating communes from one space colony or planet to the other as Earth's cities degenerate into museum pieces. Standing in the shadows of the technological revolution, our concrete and glass dormitories will be too archaic to modernize, too precious to destroy, yet too outmoded to live in.

Robert Thomas Malthus, an English curate whose theories on population growth took Europe by storm in the 1820s, predicted that the population of Europe would double every twenty-five years. Had he been right there would have been 24,000 million Europeans by 1975 instead of the actual figure of 737 million (which includes Soviet Russia and the Iron Curtain countries).

Most futurists point to hunger as one of the globe's growing concerns. There are signs the politics of food will come to rival the politics of oil.

The Futurist movement was anticipated back in the thirties when Professor A.M. Low wrote that he could "conceive the day" when Britain would have a Ministry of the Future. In an article in *Tomorrow: The Magazine of the Future* (Spring, 1938), Low assigns the Minister of the Future the very tasks futurists are accomplishing today:

> It will be the duty of the Minister to collect data from all over the world, to tabulate, correlate, compare and calculate. He will be like a spider sitting in a web, drawing towards him all knowledge, and working out, on scientific lines, the effect that the latest developments and discoveries will probably have upon the human race.

Esfandiary anticipates the transformation of society not through conflict, but through deep-seated changes in social structure — all of them precipitated by technological developments. Families will be usurped by test tube conception and a universal language will break down the last remaining communication barriers. Political left and right, so firmly rooted in today's ideologies, will disappear and leisure for all will be a by-product of ubiquitous cybernetic technology.

Prospecting for Tomorrow

There are futurists, though not many, who preach caution and even despair, and there are futurists whose predictions exceed the best we could possibly hope for. The likelihood is that Tomorrow will fall somewhere in the "L-5" between the two. Daniel Bell, former chairman of the American Academy's *Commission on the Year 2000*, summed up the futurists' median view in this list of what we can expect over the next twenty years:

- Great social, political and economic stress increasing the possibility of armed conflict.
- Accelerating economic growth.
- More leisure time, longer life and a resultant drift toward hedonism.
- A reduced labor force with a greater proportion of workers in the service occupations. Many will pursue several careers in a lifetime.
- New food and energy sources.
- A dramatic increase in the use of low-cost electronic communications.
- Man heavily committed in space.

The father of the futurists, Bertrand de Jouvenel, must be proud of the way the professional predictors have fashioned a future for themselves. Born in Paris in 1903, de Jouvenel was the inspiration behind the International Futuribles Association and was making predictions when many of today's celebrated futurists were still in rompers. Back in the winter of 1951, he delivered a report to France's leading politicians warning them that Algeria would soon revolt against the mother country. The predicted revolt broke out in October, 1954. Far from claiming gifted foresight, de Jouvenel stated he merely observed the facts and conditions around him

— the cardinal duty of the modern futurist. "Of course," remarked de Jouvenel, "there is no foresight of the future if one refuses to look at the present."

So swiftly and surely have the professional predictors established themselves that government and industry can no longer do without them. To ignore their expertise would be to risk greater uncertainty and potential for crisis. And that's something every bureaucracy and corporation, counting on smoothness and stability for success, is anxious to avoid. But the futurists do more than predict. Armed with their rationality and an optimistic point of view, they attempt to use their game plans to fashion our future. This way the predictors can, for the first time in history, prompt the fulfillment of their predictions. Not only do they say, "This could happen," they also tell us, "This should happen if we do so and so." Futurist John McHale captured the spirit of his colleagues when he said, "The fundamental realization is that man's future is literally what he chooses to make it . . . the conscious degree of control he may exercise in determining his future is quite unprecedented."

Although Fate always has the last word over rational planning, the futurists insist we are not matchwood adrift on the oceans of fortune. We can avoid the unsound and the unthinkable; we can, despite all the hazards, hammer out a destiny of daring and delight.

Months before the world learned of the political turmoil in Iran, Hudson Institute analyst George Whitman prepared a confidential report predicting the fall of the Shah and the date of his exile, as well as his replacement by a religious leader.

The Shah's exile on January 17, 1979 came within two weeks of Whitman's forecast. Two weeks later, the fanatically religious Ayatollah Khomeini took control and established an Islamic republic.

IV
INTIMATIONS OF THE END

The words of I Peter, verse 7 — "But the end of all things is at hand" — have inspired doomwatch prophets and their followers for nearly 2,000 years. In tracing the history of the doomsday obsessives, we find the lives of people who believe they're about to witness the end of the world are charged with new intensity before the big let-down.

Premonitory predictions appear to different people at different times — usually as an indication of imminent tragedy. Despite untold instances of premonitions, their source still eludes investigators.

The heading of the final chapter says it all. *From the Great Pyramid to the Cheshire Idiot* shows how bizarre and diverse prophecy can be.

History shows the doomsters' predictions never lacked an audience.

11 Doomwatch

"Doomsday is near; die all, die merrily."

William Shakespeare

"I Shall Be Released . . ."

They've waited on hilltops and in underground bunkers. They've waited at the factory bench and in the fields. They've waited long-ingly and impatiently; bravely and with fluttering stomachs; on tiptoe and on bended knee. Their hearts pounding with expectation, the prophets of doom and their followers have waited . . . and waited . . . and waited. And when the world hasn't ended after all, they've had little option but to hang their heads in disillusionment and mutter excuses about miscalculation or our unreadiness for the blessing of divine destruction. It's not easy for the prophets of doom when the sun rises on a day they vowed would never dawn. For they must descend from their hilltops or emerge from their bunkers to suffer the taunts and jeers of enduring humanity. Yet history tells us that no matter how incontrovertible the facts, the doomsters rarely admit to being wrong. Their reasoning will always help them devise ways to justify, and even strengthen, the faith that has led them to wait in vain.

The scaremongers of the apocalypse have been with us since the beginning of time, ever since man, unsure of his origins, realized that someday, somehow, we must encounter the end of it all. Bible prophecy, which tells of the second coming of Christ and the de-struction of the world as we know it, has provided endless am-munition for predictors with a penchant for the melodramatic. These alarmists indulgently place themselves and their followers in the shoes of the elect who, according to I Thessalonians 4:7, "are still alive and remain on the earth" once the earth has taken its terminal bashing. Of course, not all prophets get their inspiration from the

Bible. But there's really very little difference between the early Christian prophet Montanus, who predicted the final curtain would fall in the second century, and the more sectarian Roch "Moses" Thériault who, along with thirteen devotees and four children, holed up in a log cabin on Quebec's Gaspé peninsula to wait for the world to end on February 19, 1979.

We can make one prediction with certainty: sooner or later the doomsters must be right. Even if we rule out the possibility of vengeful intercession by the Almighty, we must face the fact that a supernova — the explosion of a star — could vaporize the earth at any time. We could be hit by a comet or asteroid which might blow our atmosphere right out into space. And we *know* the earth's lifespan cannot outlast the sun's; our benevolent star is expected to expand and scorch the earth in about 4.5 billion years, although it could happen earlier. Much earlier.

Each successive prophet who forecasts the imminent end of the world — and history has shown us hundreds — believes he's the one who knows. Despite a prophetic track record that couldn't be worse — we're still waiting, after all, for a doomwatch that's justified — there's no shortage of hopefuls willing to stake their all on predicting the Grand Finale. Like losing on lottery or raffle tickets, experience teaches us nothing. Maybe next time! With the approach of the year 2,000 — the same thing happened as the first millennium drew near — terminal predictions are being stepped up. There's a boom in doom, you might say. A recent newsletter for psychotherapists suggested that up to ten per cent of North Americans are giving the end of the world "serious consideration."

A modern expert on doomsday cults, Dr. Michael Persinger of the Department of Psychology at Laurentian University, Sudbury, Ontario, attributes their attraction to a lack of interest in conventional religion, an increasing uncertainty about the future and the developing complexity of daily life. Those obsessed with the end of the world "are usually people who feel they have very few options," says Persinger. "They find every day very painful and look forward to the Golden City."

The apocalyptic urge, it seems, is universally contagious. The downtrodden and the depressed everywhere seem to be vulnerable to the teachings of the doomsters. As Vittorio Lanternari points out in *The Religions of the Oppressed:*

Belief in the end of the world and in its regeneration, as well as in a heavenly kingdom, is the religious expression of people who yearn to break away from what holds them, and to find a new world where the forces arrayed against them will have been wiped out.

Waiting in Vain

The prophet Montanus was, in 156 A.D., one of the first to suggest the fulfillment of the apocalyptic seed planted in the Bible. Convinced the Golden City was just around the corner, he would enter a trance and utter prophecies about a heavenly Jerusalem descending to earth to signal the second coming and the world's end. He was assisted by two prophetesses, Prisca and Maximilla, in assuring his followers that the great event was destined to take place at Pepuza, near the modern Turkish city of Ankara. Montanus' disciples flocked in such numbers to the appointed spot that a new town sprang up to house them. Although the end was indefinitely postponed, the movement withstood the disappointment and outlived its prophets, even gaining enough strength to create a serious division in the Christian world. Though Montanism limped on into the fifth century, it couldn't survive the destruction of its fundamental precept.

In the third century, a prophet called Novatian gathered a huge following in the Mediterranean countries. "Come, Lord Christ," his followers cried, "clothed in all thy wrath and judgment, come with all thy vengeance, come!"

Donatus, who came from North Africa, commanded fervent attention in the fourth century. He was the first prophet to stress that only 144,000 people would be chosen by God. He found his magic figure in the Book of Revelation (14:1) which says: ". . . and, lo, a Lamb stood on the mount Sion, and with him an hundred forty and four thousand, having his Father's name written in their foreheads." In this century, the Jehovah's Witnesses, while carefully refraining from picking a date for Judgment Day, likewise believe that heavenly privileges will be granted to the world's most righteous 144,000. Branded as heretics by the established church, Novatian and Donatus came and went, but the apocalyptic embers still smoldered . . .

As the year 1,000 approached, Europe was seized by the feverish conviction that the last days had finally arrived. Churches were packed with the newly repentant and the populations of towns and villages assembled around huge crucifixes under the open sky. Although the first millennium passed without anything extraordinary happening, superstition and irrational beliefs remained. By the year 1186, the Byzantine Emperor walled up the windows of his Constantinople palace, the Archbishop of Canterbury proclaimed a national fast of atonement, the German people dug scores of doomsday shelters and in Persia and Mesopotamia, believers repaired to their cellars in readiness for the end of the world as foreseen by an anonymous astrologer who signed himself John of Toledo. Though time proved him wrong, people were ready for more of the same. Religious historian Marcus Bach wrote, "Anabaptists, Waldensians, Albigenses, Moravian Brethren, Swiss Brethren, became links in an unbroken chain of apocalyptical advocates."

The Dutch Anabaptists believed the end would come in 1533, and as acceptance for this prediction grew, church congregations prepared to meet their Maker. Historian Richard Heath tells how:

> They sought to exemplify equality and brotherhood in their lives. Well-to-do Brothers and Sisters gave all their wealth to the poor, destroyed their rent rolls, forgave their debtors, renounced worldly pleasures, studying to live an unwordly life.

Yet when 1534 rolled around, few Anabaptists considered they had been swindled out of their goods. They continued whipping faith and conviction to new heights of enthusiasm . . . for a time.

In the seventeenth century a prophet called Sabbatai Zevi led the most comical of all the doomster charades. Born in the Turkish town of Smyrna, he grew up leading a monastic life, devoting all his time and energy to studying the Cabala. Although he was only twenty years old, he gathered around him a group of disciples to whom he granted insight into the book's mysteries. But then he went a step further. He let his followers into the secret that *he* was the one they were waiting for: the promised Messiah. The Jews of the day were looking toward 1648 as the year of the second coming, yet it wasn't until this year had passed that Zevi publicly declared himself the Messiah. The result was as swift as it was unwelcome: Zevi and his disciples were kicked out of Smyrna.

Strangely enough, this was only the beginning. For Zevi then latched onto another popular date for the end of time — 1666 — and traveled from city to city in the Near East, exhorting people to accept him as the Chosen One. In spite of, or perhaps because of, opposition from established Jewry, those eager for salvation scrambled to his side. Soon Zevi's name was being proclaimed all over the Jewish world, and in 1665, popular feeling was running so high that he was allowed to return to Smyrna where the locals welcomed him like a lost son. Zevi and his followers then set out for Constantinople in a bid to fulfill the prediction that the Sultan would be deposed to prepare the way for the return of the exiled Jews to the Holy Land. But Zevi and company badly bungled their campaign. They were arrested as soon as they landed on the shores of the Dardanelles and the Messiah was led in chains to a jail near Constantinople.

At first Zevi's followers were subdued by this setback, but soon they came to hold the opinion that their leader's imprisonment represented the suffering necessary for his true calling. Once more his popularity soared as thousands gathered beneath the jail walls in hopes of glimpsing the man they believed would save them. H. Graetz in *History of the Jews* describes how Jews in various parts of Europe made ready to head back to Israel under Zevi's leadership:

> In Hungary they began to unroof their houses. In large, commercial cities, where Jews took the lead in wholesale business, such as Amsterdam, Leghorn and Hamburg, stagnation of trade ensued.

Wanting least of all to make a martyr out of Zevi, the Sultan tried to convert him to Islam, and to his own and everyone else's amazement, he succeeded. There was the Messiah wearing the turban of the opposition as his devotees clamored for his release and the promotion of his glory! The news that their savior had become just another Moslem must have been difficult for the faithful to accept. Most reacted by trying to forget their devotion to the turncoat prophet. Others, however, demonstrating how flexible those who yearn to believe can be, became Moslems, too. And so the movement of Sabbatai Zevi sputtered to a halt.

As the world's horizons widened, so the prophets of doom cast their spells over ever greater parts of the globe. America, a land of freedom where there was plenty of room to escape the strictures of traditional belief, drew the apocalyptically inclined from across the Atlantic in substantial numbers. Word got around: there was no place like the New World to greet the end of the world. One of the United States' first doomwatch communes was set up in the Pennsylvania wilderness by a group known as The Woman in the Wilderness. The group's founder, Johann Jacob Zimmerman, forecast

The world is doomed — but not for at least another twenty-five billion years, according to Jack Hills, a theoretical astrophysicist at Michigan State University.

Hills predicts the end will arrive when Earth becomes a super-snack for a massive "black hole." All the suns and planets and gasses floating around the Milky Way will be gobbled up likewise.

A black hole is a vast invisible body which is so dense and has such tremendous gravity that nothing — not even light rays — can escape it.

The black hole that feeds on Earth will have the mass of 300 million suns and will swallow whole stars effortlessly, says Hills whose September, 1979 prediction came from his study on colliding stars, funded by the National Science Foundation.

But he reckons the celestial bodies won't begin to disappear for another 25 to 40 billion years — an eternity roughly twice the estimated age of the known universe.

the world would end in the fall of 1694. He, at least, wasn't disappointed: he died on the day his followers set sail in February of that year. Zimmerman had decided a wilderness setting would be best to greet the returning Messiah, taking his lead from the Book of Revelation that described a woman who was given "two wings of a great eagle, that she might fly into the wilderness, into her place, where she is nourished for a time, and times and a half time from the face of the serpent." Hence the name, The Woman in the Wilderness. Once established under new leadership in Pennsylvania, the group built a wooden tabernacle with a roof telescope so the members could better observe the signs of the end. But when the world survived the fall of 1694, the little community's pulse slackened perceptibly. Things were never quite the same again. By 1750, the Woman in the Wilderness was no more.

The Rappites were a convivial bunch who established a number of thriving communities in the early days of the United States. Although they believed the end of the world was imminent, they didn't waste time waiting for it. They went at life with joy and enthusiasm, building and operating, among other things, the Golden Rule Distillery which was renowned for its whisky. "Father" George Rapp, who arrived in America from Germany in 1804 as leader of the Rappites, was convinced the second coming of Christ would happen before he died. As he lay on his death bed at the age of ninety, he was still confident he'd soon play the role of mediator of the apocalypse. His last words to his supporters were, "If I did not know that the dear Lord meant I should present you all to him, I should think my last moments come."

No apocalyptic group gave America a greater scare than the Millerites, a movement started practically against the will of its founder, farmer William Miller from New York State. After two years of long nights spent poring over his Bible — in particular the Book of Daniel which talks of the "sanctuary" being "cleansed" after "two thousand and three hundred days" — Miller convinced himself the world would be destroyed by fire in 1843. He arrived at this conclusion by tracing the authorship of the Book of Daniel back to 456 B.C. and converting Biblical "days" into human years. For several years Miller kept quiet about his calculations, until the time he received an invitation to lecture on Bible prophecy. That lecture did it. Miller's views were passed around and a movement was in the making. By 1840, hundreds of thousands of people living along the eastern seaboard had put their faith in the prophet of doom. In the

When the final day comes, most prophets of doom believe, they and their followers will be among those to survive.

spring of 1842, a convention was held in Boston and the delegates voted to accept the following resolution:

> *Resolved,* that in the opinion of this conference, there are most serious and important reasons for believing that God has revealed the time of the end of the world, and that that time is 1843.

Newspapers such as *Signs of the Times* in Boston, *The Midnight Cry* in New York and *The Philadelphia Alarm* spread the word as

The world didn't end on Christmas Day, 1973, but Edward Elson, the man who sold tickets for a spaceship ride to escape the catastrophe, was not disappointed.

"I don't want to see the end of the world," he said on Boxing Day. "It's just a revelation that came to me and I gave voice to it."

Elson, a lawyer from McFarland, Wisconsin, had announced that before the world ended, the comet Kohoutek would act as a spaceship and rescue a select few. According to his revelation, Kohoutek would then mix with the earth's atmosphere, sending the world "down in a sea of petroleum oil."

Elson said he was selected to choose 1,000 people for the spaceship ride. He had 1,000 tickets printed that he sold to buy his wife jewels to entice her aboard the ship. But his wife's skepticism remained unshaken.

people rushed to the altar of Millerism. Early in 1843, a tabernacle was built in Boston, and its opening drew a capacity crowd of 3,500. As the year ticked away, Miller published a synopsis of his beliefs, both extending and placing limits on the day of reckoning:

> I believe the time can be known by all who desire to understand and to be ready for His coming. And I am fully convinced that sometime between March 21st., 1843 and March 21st., 1844, according to the Jewish mode of computation, Christ will come, and bring all His saints with Him; and that then He will reward every man as his work shall be.
>
> *Signs of the Times,* January 25, 1843

And so the Millerites waited and hoped until March 22, 1844, when non-believers poured scorn on their heads:

> If any of Miller's followers walked abroad, they ran the gauntlet of merciless ridicule.
>
> "What! — Not gone up yet? — We thought you'd gone up! Aren't you going up soon? — Wife didn't go up and leave you behind to burn, did she?"
>
> The rowdy element in the community would not leave them alone.
>
> (C.E. Sears, *Days of Delusion — A Strange Bit of History*)

Nevertheless, the flagging movement enjoyed a spectacular revival when a new date — October 22, 1844 — was selected for Judgment Day. Fashioning burning conviction out of tattered hopes, the revival quickly mustered more enthusiastic support than the original. *The Advent Herald* of October 20, 1844 told how many, sensing the onset of redemption, turned away from worldly chores:

> Some, on going into their fields to cut grass, found themselves entirely unable to proceed, and, conforming to their sense of duty, left their crops standing in the field to show their faith by their works, and thus to condemn the world. This rapidly extended through the north of New England.

The fervor was stoked up all the way to midnight on October 22. One man donned a pair of turkey wings, climbed to the top of a tree and prayed for the Lord to take him up. "He tried to fly, fell, and broke his arm," recounts a contemporary diarist. When midnight struck, the Millerites plummeted from the peak of ecstatic expectation to the depths of irreconcilable disappointment. This time there was no reviving the faithful. It was Millerism, not the world, that was doomed. Lamented an ex-disciple:

> Everyone felt lonely, with hardly a desire to speak to anyone. Still in the cold world! No deliverance — the Lord had not come!

Wrote another:

> Our fondest hopes and expectations were blasted, and such a spirit of weeping came over us . . . We wept, and wept until the day dawned.

Doomsday prophets have also emerged among the North American Indians. Members of the Earth Lodge cult of central California, which developed around 1870, dug underground shelters with long corridors and circular chambers to seal them from the cataclysms they felt sure would soon herald the end of the world. A similar group called the Warm House cult thrived on Oregon reservations where the shelters were square instead of round, with a hearth for a centerpiece. Both branches of this doctrine were convinced the dead would be resurrected at world's end.

Fear of doomsday also inspired the Tupinamba and Guarani tribes of Brazil to undertake mass migrations across South America in search of a paradisiacal refuge from destruction. Needless to say, they never found what they were looking for, although it certainly wasn't for lack of trying. The Tupinambas started one of their arduous treks in 1539, traveling nine years across the widest part of the continent until they reached Chachapoyas in Peru. All they found were gold-hungry Spaniards anxious for tips on how to locate a paradise of a different kind: El Dorado.

In Viet Nam, followers of the prophet Huynh Phy So abandoned their fields to await the end on a hilltop when fighting broke out between French colonists and the invading Japanese during World War Two. Central African supplicants of the Bashilele cult, which reached its zenith in the mid-1930s, stopped working in expectation of the end of the world which, they believed, would bring a liberating Messiah and the return of the dead bearing untold riches. By way of encouragement, secret rituals were held around the ancestral tombs — all to no avail.

A near-illiterate but extraordinarily persuasive laborer named Alexander Bedward took Jamaica by storm in 1920 with the launching of a doomsday cult based on himself. The movement was called

Science-fiction writer William Tenn predicts that should extra-terrestrials visit our planet, the end of humanity will swiftly follow. ". . . they'll crush us with feelings of superiority," he says.

Bedwardism and its devotees accepted Bedward's prophecy that he would ascend to heaven, later to return to destroy the earth by fire. When his ascension predicted for December 31, 1920 didn't happen, Bedward announced that the Almighty had simply granted the unfaithful more time to earn eternal salvation. Shortly thereafter, he was arrested and committed to a lunatic asylum, but his followers hung on to their redemptive dreams.

The ways of the Hawaiian prophetess Hapu were much like those of Bedward. She founded a cult in 1825 that promised destruction for all who shunned her claim that she sat alongside Jehovah and Jesus in the Holy Trinity. When she died, her body was dressed up like a pagan idol and laid in a sanctuary reserved for Hawaiian warriors. Convinced the world would end before much longer, Hapu's followers gave up their work and built a temple in honor of the prophetess. But the cult declined when the long-awaited cataclysm stubbornly refused to take place, a decline hastened by local missionaries who burned down the temple.

The Need for the End
People today are as willing as ever to believe that theirs is the generation that will witness civilization's last gasp. Since 1934, the California-based Worldwide Church of God has been churning out dire predictions to awe-struck audiences with the regularity of a bottle factory. Headed by deans of doom Garner Ted Armstrong and his father Herbert W. Armstrong, the movement has issued several end-of-the-line warnings through the magazine *Plain Truth*. And yet we're still around, still bombarded by the Armstrongs' death-wish.

In 1955, *Plain Truth* declared, ". . . we will be totally consumed and carried away captive to other nations as slaves within 20 years." In 1956, the elder Armstrong wrote in the same magazine that famine, plague and World War Three were prophesied "for 15 to 20 years or less," and in 1957 readers were told "God prophesies that finally, within the next 15 years, fully one-third of our whole population will die of disease and famine."

When Indian astrologers announced that a conjunction of all the planets in Capricorn would destroy the earth on February 5, 1962, there were outbreaks of panic not only in India, but all over the world. Brahmin holy men led a non-stop prayer session for nine days and half a million pilgrims hastened to take their last dip in the sacred Ganges at Benares. And in England's Lake District a little group bundled up in windbreakers and picked their way to the top of Mount Coniston to pray that the disaster be averted.

The 450 members of the True Light Church of Christ, based in North and South Carolina, believed the end would come in 1970. They built their forecast on the theory that the world was to last 6,000 years from the date of creation which they placed at 4,000 B.C., believing also that thirty years had been lost from the first century of the Christian calendar. This meant zero hour would arrive sometime during 1970. On New Year's Day, 1971, H. Flake Braswell, an elder of the sect, was quoted in the *New York Times* as saying: "I can't give you no satisfactory explanation."

Housepainter and clairvoyant John Nash announced that God would punish sinners by destroying the Australian city of Adelaide with a giant tidal wave and earthquake at noon on January 19, 1976. While believers fled to the hills, skeptics — among them South Australian Premier Don Dunstan — lounged on the beach as the predicted monster wave managed to lift the surf an ignominious six inches. Elsewhere, tension mounted in the hours before midday; churches were packed, liquor store tills chattered merrily away, massage parlors offered "tidal wave specials" and bikini-clad girls skipped along the beach bearing a sign urging, "Sin now — tomorrow it will be too late." Meanwhile, believers pointed fearfully to what they considered a sure sign of impending calamity: local snails were crawling to the rooftops. Nash the prophet didn't take any chances. He moved his family to Melbourne, 450 miles away.

Two and a half years later, seventy followers of the man who wrote a book called *The Doomsday Globe* took refuge in a "doomsday city" on a remote Australian ranch equipped with underground bunkers and a year's supply of food. The group, which included businessmen, pharmacists and schoolteachers, paid $575 each for what they considered to be the best chance of surviving the fulfillment of John Strong's prophecies. In his book, Strong, a forty-one year old Melbourne businessman, argued that the Soviet Union would launch a nuclear attack on the Western world sometime in October, 1978. His forecast was founded on a mixture of Bible testimony and his own calculations based on the size of the Great Pyramid of Egypt. Once again, the scoffers had a field day.

But after Canadian psychic Winnifred Barton forecast on radio and television that the world would end at 9 p.m. on June 13, 1976, even unbelievers caught themselves muttering a hasty prayer or two, just in case. On the stroke of the predicted hour of doom,

Twentieth century
doomwatch: Roch "Moses"
Thériault and Chantale
Labrie pictured in their
Gaspé retreat.

Toronto's buildings were shaken by loud claps of thunder, lightning zig-zagged across the sky and the fearful reached for their telephones to ask police department officials whether it was, in truth, the end of the world. "We had dozens of calls from very frightened people," said an unflappable Toronto police spokesman. "We asked them to call us back at 9:05."

February 19, 1979 was the date Roch "Moses" Thériault set for the end of the world. With his devoted band of thirteen disciples and four children, Moses, aged thirty-two, settled in a log cabin retreat on an isolated lump of land christened "the eternal mountain" on Quebec's Gaspé peninsula. For four months leading up to February 19, the little group sat out the rigors of the Canadian winter . . . and they continued to sit tight even after the dread deadline had passed. In April, however, the parents of twenty-one year old Chantale Labrie, one of the "Holy Moses Mountain Family" as they'd been dubbed, obtained a court order enabling police to bring her in for psychiatric observation. When the law arrived by helicopter to retrieve her, Thériault protested and was airlifted out, too — on a charge of obstructing police. After pleading guilty, he was discharged with a one year suspended sentence and Miss Labrie was freed after tests showed she was mentally sound. But these tangles with officialdom didn't seem to deter the little group. At the time of writing, they are reunited on the eternal mountain. The end of the world had been postponed but not, presumably, canceled. While the group waits for eternity, its members tolerate the intrusion from time to time of a visitor from the place that used to be called home, as long as the outsiders remove all jewelery, leave behind any tobacco and drugs and refrain from swearing. "We've got nothing against our birth relatives coming for a visit," said Esther, Moses' disciple and common-law wife, "as long as they don't try to take us away from our lives for God."

The great seductiveness of the doomsday prophets lies in their offer of release to those without love, hope or purpose. How marvelous it would be to wipe the slate clean! How purging, how purifying to be blown to smithereens along with this sad old world! As with suicide, oblivion is the aim — the end of day-to-day difficulties, the end of problems with relationships, work and school. The end of striving. "One might think," writes Daniel Cohen in *Voodoo, Devils and the New Invisible World*, "that since the end of the world has been predicted so many times, people have become a little bored and suspicious with new prophecies. Some people have, but I venture to guess that the apocalyptic urge is about as strong today as it ever was."

The sudden landslide at Aberfan, in Wales, was the subject of more than one premonition.

12 Premonitions

Premonition: 1. previous warning, notice, or information: FOREWARNING. 2. anticipation of an event without conscious reason: PRESENTIMENT.

Webster's Dictionary

"When someone purports to have knowledge of the future which goes beyond the normal . . . our instinctive tendency is to dismiss him without a second thought. Perhaps we need to be more charitable."

Frederick R. Struckmeyer

"There's No Explanation for It."

Ten nights in a row, twenty-three year old David Booth had the same fiery nightmare. First, he heard the sound of faltering engines. Then he watched in horror as a huge American Airlines plane banked steeply to one side before rolling over and crashing to earth in a ball of red and orange flame. So vivid was the dream that not only did Booth see the crash and hear the explosion, he felt the heat of the fire, too. Shaken awake by this recurring vision, he was dogged for the rest of the day by fear, frustration and depression. Sometimes, he cried.

After several nights, Booth, an office manager for a car rental company, could no longer keep the horror to himself. He telephoned the Federal Aviation Administration offices at the Greater Cincinnati Airport. Then he called American Airlines and a psychiatrist at the University of Cincinnati. The calls, made on Tuesday, May 22, 1979, were received attentively, but the sympathetic response didn't make David Booth feel any better. The following Friday, after ten nights of nightmares, he was nearly mad with helplessness and anxiety. That was the evening he learned an American Airlines DC-10 had crashed on take-off from Chicago's O'Hare International Airport in the worst air disaster in North American history. Two hundred and seventy-three people were killed.

The news came as no surprise to David Booth. "There was never any doubt to me that something was going to happen," he said. "It wasn't like a dream. It was like I was standing there watching the whole thing — like watching television." Earlier, officials at the FAA offices had vainly tried to match the details of his nightmare

An Eastern Airlines stewardess working the New York-Miami run had a premonition of a jumbo jet crashing, left wing first, into the water at night. She "heard" the cries of the injured and was left with "a weird, sick feeling," thinking the crash would happen around New Year's Day. Two weeks later, on December 29, 1972, a last-minute change in her schedule prevented her from boarding the night flight from New York to Miami. At 11:42 p.m., the aircraft crashed, left wing first, into the Florida Everglades, killing 79 people out of the 180 aboard.

with an airport or airplane somewhere in the nation. When they heard about the crash they remembered his advance description only too well. "It was uncanny," said Jack Barker, public affairs officer for the FAA's southern region. "There were differences, but there were very many similarities. The greatest similarity was his calling the airline and the airplane . . . and that it [the plane] came in inverted." Booth, he explained, had mentioned a "three engine aircraft" resembling the DC-10, and his description of the crash site was similar to the Chicago airport.

Although Booth's nightmares stopped once the crash had taken place, his feelings of helplessness remained. "How can you make any sense of something like that?" he asked. "There's no explanation for it. No meaning. No conclusion. It just doesn't make any sense."

David Booth is not the only one who's been asking himself that question. No one really knows how or why premonitions happen, not even researchers who've worked at cracking the ciphers of parapsychological phenomena. Nor does anyone really know why some people and not others act as "receivers." There's certainly no lack of examples of premonitory awareness, and while we do know some people "see" or "sense" an event before it happens, the debate about premonitions and where they come from is far from over. Dr. Ian Stevenson of the University of Virginia, an experienced and respected premonition investigator, brings us a little closer to understanding the mystery. He suggests premonitions occur when the barrier separating the conscious and unconscious divisions of the mind suddenly breaks down. When this takes place, a person is granted a glimpse of his or other people's life plan. This wonderful — and sometimes terrifying — process happens in the uncharted regions of the mind, and we can only watch its results from the outside.

Accounts of premonitions are scattered throughout history, as far back and further than Socrates (469-399 B.C.) who, according to Xenophon, said, "I have told my friends the warnings I have received, and up to now the voice has never been wrong." Very often, but not always, premonitions bring notice of bad news. Usually, but not necessarily, they are projected in dreams with a cinematic realism like that of David Booth's nightmares. But just as often, intimations of the future can penetrate a person's being without images, leaving a feeling of abiding unease or a sensation, linked to a person or place, that *something* is going to happen. Sometimes the sense of impending disaster is so strong that the receiver becomes physically ill.

Titanic and Aberfan

Back in 1898, writer Morgan Robertson made use of a particularly eerie disaster premonition by crafting it into a novel. Robertson, who specialized in stories of ships and the sea, was the kind of writer who waited for inspiration. Sometimes he lounged around for days in his New York studio before the required mood settled in. On this

A novelist, a churchman, a second engineer, a psychic and many more had premonitions that the "unsinkable" Titanic would be lost.

Tobacco planter Robert Morris Sr. — the father of the financier of the American Revolution — dreamed he'd be killed by the firing of a cannon from a ship he was about to visit. He tried to avoid boarding the vessel, but his fears appeared so unfounded that he finally yielded to the captain's entreaties, once he'd been assured no guns would be fired until he'd left. At the end of the visit, the captain told Morris the saluting shot would be fired only when Morris' party had safely reached the shore. He told his gunners not to fire the salute until he raised his hand. But the boat carrying Morris to shore was still within range when the captain raised a hand to brush a fly off his nose. This was interpreted as the signal to fire and the gun was discharged; a fragment hit Robert Morris, wounding him fatally.

occasion, when the Muse at last called him to the typewriter, he felt so inspired that the story practically wrote itself. He sat down, possessed by a powerful image of an 800 foot long luxury liner speeding through the fog that hung over the iceberg-strewn North Atlantic. Then he tapped out these words:

> She was the largest craft afloat and the greatest of the works of men . . . spacious cabins . . . decks like broad promenades . . . Unsinkable, indestructible, she carried as few lifeboats as would satisfy the laws . . .
>
> Seventy five thousand tons — deadweight — rushing through the fog at the rate of fifty feet a second . . . hurled itself at an iceberg . . . nearly 3,000 human voices, raised in agonized screams . . .

Robertson called his book *The Wreck of the Titan*. Thirteen years later, the "unsinkable" luxury liner *Titanic* was built and on April 10, 1912, the pride of the English shipyards sailed from Southampton on her maiden voyage across the Atlantic. At 11:59 p.m. on Monday, April 15, the *Titanic* ground into an iceberg and sank at a steep angle, drowning 1,493 of the 2,207 passengers and crew. So many are the similarities between Robertson's novel and the real-life tragedy that coincidence has to be ruled out. Common to both were the name of the ship, the Atlantic, the iceberg, the fog, the liner's myth of unsinkability, the length and tonnage, the number of passengers, the speed of impact, the number of lifeboats and propellers and the unprecedented loss of life. Morgan Robertson had had a premonition without even knowing it, but he wasn't the only one to be warned of what the film industry was to call "A Night to Remember."

Ten years before Robertson's novel appeared, W.T. Stead wrote a story that was published in the *Pall Mall Gazette* about a giant liner that sank in mid-Atlantic. "This is exactly what might take place and what will take place," he concluded, "if liners are sent to sea short of boats." The *Titanic*, by the way, capable of carrying 3,500 passengers and crew, had lifeboats for only 950. In 1910, Stead gave a lecture in London in which he pictured himself shipwrecked, struggling in the water and shouting for help. Next, psychic Count Louis Hamon warned him that travel would be dangerous in the month of April, 1912. An American woman wrote to *Light* magazine saying a voice had told her Stead would be "called home" in the "first half of 1912." And Stead himself received a letter from a churchman predicting the sinking of the *Titanic*. In spite of this overwhelming premonitory evidence, Stead, having been invited to America by President William Taft to speak at a peace conference, booked a passage on the vessel and was one of the many who lost their lives.

Others acted more cautiously, following their hunches or the many warning signs. A premonition caused Colin Macdonald to turn down an offer of a post as second engineer on the *Titanic*. Several people, including banker J. Pierpont Morgan, canceled their passages in the week before embarkation, giving the excuse that it was unlucky to sail on a maiden voyage. And on the day of the sailing, psychic V.N. Turvey warned that a great liner would be lost. Those who felt uneasy about the voyage, yet who allowed their rational mind to still their fears, would surely have panicked could they have witnessed the antics of a woman named Mrs. Marshall who, from her rooftop on the Isle of Wight, followed the liner's progress out into the English Channel. As she gazed across the water, she suddenly became hysterical. "It's going to sink!" she cried. "That ship is going to sink before she reaches America!" Her family could do nothing to calm her as she went on to describe the doomed travelers struggling in the icy waters. And then, as the liner dwindled to a dot on the horizon, Mrs. Marshall, living the passengers' terrifying future, started to shout. "Save them!" she cried. "Save them!"

Nothing attracts premonitions like a massive disaster that should never have happened. Just as the logical mind could not have conceived of the "unsinkable" *Titanic* going down on her maiden voyage, so it was unthinkable that half a million tons of coal waste loosened by two days of heavy rain would slide down an 800 foot slag heap onto a school in a South Wales mining village and kill twenty-eight adults and one hundred sixteen children. But that's exactly what happened at Aberfan on October 21, 1966. Once more, all the presentiments of death were there for those who could understand them. But, as with David Booth's recurring nightmare, who could be sure what these disturbing sensations really meant?

Few got the message as clearly as little Eryl Mai Jones, but her nine years worked against her. It's difficult for an adult to translate a premonition into a clear warning; for a child it's well nigh impossible. Nobody took her seriously when she said on the morning before the tragedy, "I dreamed I went to school and there was no school there. Something black had come down all over it." Two weeks earlier, Eryl Mai had spoken very strangely for such a young

Birds and animals have premonitions, too.

On the afternoon of August 17, 1959, thousands of gulls, terns and other water fowl flapped away from Montana's Lake Hegben after a stay of several months. Hours later, the mystery of their mass departure was solved when earthquakes rocked the area, springing cracks in the Hegben Dam and causing a flood that killed several local residents and Yellowstone Park tourists. But the birds and animals were safe. Not one animal carcass was reported to the government wildlife services.

The wildlife must have acted on a warning. Dr. J.B. Rhine noted in 1951 in the *Journal of Parapsychology* that there are "a fair number of cases in which the animals' reaction is taken to be premonitory." Exactly what they are reacting to is another matter altogether.

girl. "Mummy, I'm not afraid to die," she said. "I shall be with Peter and June." At the mass funeral for the victims of Pantglas Junior School on October 25, Eryl Mai was buried between her classmates, Peter and June.

Psychiatrist Dr. John Barker later appealed through a London newspaper for any premonitions about the Aberfan disaster. Of seventy-six replies, he considered sixty were worthy of investigation. He was able to confirm twenty-four of these either through corroboration from witnesses or from seeing evidence that the premonition had been recorded before the disaster. We'll include just a few examples of the messages people received across Great Britain as the countdown to Aberfan neared its climax . . .

Early on October 21, an elderly man living in northwest England was startled by a dream in which the letters A-B-E-R-F-A-N were spelled out in bright lights. He had no idea what the letters meant until he listened to the radio later that day. The night before, Mrs. C. Milden, attending a meeting of Spiritualists in Plymouth, Devon, had a terrifying vision of a landslide rushing down a mountain toward a school. She visualized rescue workers digging into the mounds of slag, searching for bodies. Close by stood a terrified boy with a long fringe and a rescue worker with a strange peaked cap. While watching TV coverage of the rescue operations three days later she saw exactly the same scene, with the man and the boy appearing precisely as they had in her premonition. Another woman had a vision of schoolchildren going to heaven dressed in Welsh national costume, while yet another warning was spelled out by "hundreds of black horses thundering down a hillside dragging hearses."

Premonition Bureaux

The fact that premonitions can warn us of impending disaster begs the question: can't we use this instinct to avert natural and man-made calamities? This was the very concern that led to the formation of the British Premonitions Bureau in January, 1967. In June, 1968 a similar organization — the Central Premonitions Registry — was founded in New York. These offices awaited word from people who experienced twitches and flashes of approaching disaster, and they responded eagerly. As expected, the authentic premonitions had to be sifted from a mass of "unexpressed fears or unfulfilled desires" that all dreams are said to express. But among the throng of misses there proved to be a few direct hits. The British bureau (which closed down in 1977 to be replaced, in 1979, by a London office run by the magazine *Alpha*) received four amazingly accurate predictions of Robert Kennedy's assassination. The New York bureau has had its successes, too. On May 12, 1969, New York resident Thomas Casas forwarded the following premonition:

> In my dream I saw what appeared to be a Piper-type plane. The rudder was painted blue and the number [of the plane] was N 129 N, N 429 N, or N 29 N . . . I saw the craft make a bumpy landing, and the craft nosed over. The door opened and the pilot sprawled on the ground.

On August 31, 1969, undefeated heavyweight boxing champion Rocky Marciano was killed in a plane crash in Iowa. The airplane was a light, Piper-type craft. Painted on its fuselage was the serial number N 3149 X — not far from the image seen by Casas.

Early in the spring of 1972, a woman sent in this message: "Governor George Wallace is going to be shot . . . at a rally . . . as he steps off a stage."

A few weeks later — on May 15, 1972 — Wallace was shot four times as he walked from his bullet-proof podium at a Laurel, Mary-

"Governor George Wallace is going to be shot . . . at a rally . . . as he steps off a stage."

German predictor and astronomer Johannes Kepler (1571-1630) uttered six Latin words which came to be known as the prophecy of the six Ms. They were *Magnus Monarchis Matthias Menso Martis Morietur* (the great monarch, Matthias, will die in the month of March). The Emperor Matthias died in March, 1619.

land shopping center. Wallace survived, but he was paralyzed by a bullet that lodged near his spinal column. On the night of the shooting, the woman who'd predicted the Governor's fate telephoned Robert D. Nelson, director of the premonitions registry, and exclaimed, "My God, it really happened! I'm afraid to go to bed and dream again." Nelson did his best to soothe her, and he encouraged her to continue dreaming because, as he put it, "It's just possible that some day a lady like this is going to avert a tragedy."

But the premonition bureaux have yet to accomplish their life-saving mission. The trouble is that so many premonitions lack the essential coordinates of time and place, and people with the authority to act are often loath to even consider these warnings for fear of giving in to the "kooky" side of the human mind. But Nelson won't fail for lack of trying. "If I got three or four letters advising me the president was going to be in a plane crash on a certain day," he said, "I would not hesitate to pick up the phone, call the White House and advise his people of the hunch."

By 1979, two new premonition bureaux had been opened in California in hopes that "human seismographs" would deliver early warnings to minimize the death toll when the next monster earthquake shakes the San Andreas Fault. One of the bureau's founders, English psychic researcher Dr. Douglas Dean of Newark College of Engineering, New Jersey, sees precognition as California's only effective defence against the next big quake. "Analysis of the Aberfan premonitions showed that there was a gradual build-up for about a week before it happened," he said. "If we can monitor earthquake premonitions then we should be able to see the gradual increase and give warning before the peak."

Although history holds out little chance of success for the plan, Nicholas Wotton, Dean of Canterbury, proved back in 1553 that premonitions, if heeded, can be extremely useful. More than once, Wotton dreamed that his nephew, Thomas Wotton, was about to become entangled in a scheme that would ruin the family name and cost Thomas his life. So the Dean, who was also ambassador to France, wrote to Queen Mary asking her to commit his nephew to prison for a reason he would later explain. While Thomas was incarcerated, the Queen learned of a plot to prevent her imminent marriage to King Philip of Spain. It turned out that young Wotton, had he been free, would have been among the conspirators. As it was, he sat in his cell, guiltless and more than a little relieved as the plotters were apprehended, tried and executed. Uncle had saved his life.

It was more tragic for Abraham Lincoln. He had no way of knowing how to escape the fulfillment of the premonition that foretold his death. Lincoln's dream came but a few days before his assassination at Ford's Theatre. On April 11, 1865, three days before the murder, Colonel Ward H. Lamon, a lawyer and White House aide, jotted down an account of the dream given that day by the President himself:

> I went from room to room; no living person was in sight, but the same mournful sounds of distress met me as I passed along . . . I kept on until I arrived at the East Room, which I entered. There I met with a sickening surprise. Before me was a catafalque, on which rested a corpse wrapped in funeral vestments . . . "Who is dead in the White House?" I demanded of one of the soldiers. "The president," was his answer; "He was killed by an assassin!"

Abraham Lincoln. The President had visions of his own death.

Heads of state, who intrude so forcefully into the public mind, have always figured prominently in premonitions. Television enables people to "dream" about our leaders, knowing clearly what they look like. President John F. Kennedy's sheer visual impact may have been largely responsible for the plethora of premonitions associated with his assassination on November 22, 1963. Even this writer's mother dreamed the night before that a gunman burst into the White House and sprayed the walls with bullets. But familiarity with a subject, no matter how it may enhance a visual image, is most definitely *not* a prerequisite for the premonition itself.

This was demonstrated back in May, 1812, when John Williams, an innkeeper from Redruth, Cornwall, "saw" the shooting of an important Parliamentary figure in the lobby of the House of Commons. He had the same vivid dream three nights in succession without recognizing any of the participants; since he lived so far from London, he'd never seen any of the politicians of his day. But when he recounted the dream to his son-in-law, a frequent visitor to London, Mr. Williams was shocked to learn his description of the "murdered" man fit British Prime Minister Spencer Perceval. A few days later, a passenger stepped off the stagecoach from London with the news that Perceval had been shot and killed in the lobby of the Commons in precisely the manner Williams had foretold.

So far, we've dealt exclusively with premonitions that foreshadow disaster. But cheerful, even profitable, events can be sensed, too. Take the case of the London newspaper typesetter who dreamed of the horse destined to win the Epsom Derby of 1876. In his dream he was handed an urgent slip of copy for setting. It read: "The winner of the Derby has now received a name. It is Kisber." So realistic was the message that the man leafed through the next morning's paper in search of the enigmatic Kisber. He couldn't find that name, but he did locate an unnamed entry owned by Alexander Baltazzi, a Hungarian nobleman. Following his hunch, the typesetter placed as much money as he could on the horse with no name. How happy he must have been to learn the horse was belatedly named Kisber and that it had beaten the favorite, Petrach, by several lengths!

The Laws of Probability

When a premonition is voiced and then fails to happen, who, or what, is to blame? Has the premonition been misinterpreted? Or is it a case of an accurately received message being annuled by unforeseen developments? These questions are still unanswered in the case of the unfulfilled prediction that a tremor at Terrapin Point, Niagara Falls would cause the retaining wall to collapse, sinking the tour boat *Maid of the Mist* as it entered the whirlpool beneath the Falls at 4:56 p.m. on Sunday, July 22, 1979. Drawn by the publicity, hundreds flocked to the Falls on the fateful day and glanced anxiously at their watches as the *Maid of the Mist* braved the frothy, churning water near the foot of the Falls at precisely 4:56 . . . But nothing extraordinary happened. The Falls didn't fall, nobody was hurt and both predictor — housewife Pat St. John from Bridgewater, Connecticut — and her prediction were showered with scorn. The Jehovah's Witnesses, who were holding a convention in the resort town at the time, went so far as to say Mrs. St. John was possessed by the devil.

Yet all the signs were that the "devil woman" was onto something. At first, engineers dispatched to inspect the rock formation and other structures around the Falls found all was as it should be. But two weeks after the prediction was made public, a seismic alarm sounded, indicating the rock at Terrapin Point had shifted at least a quarter of an inch. The alarm brought on the cancellation of the *Maid of the Mist* boat rides and the Cave of the Winds walkway tours along the base of the Falls, and they remained canceled until geologists and engineers assured the public that the rockface was "apparently stable." Officials admitted, however, that a rockslide could happen at the Falls "in five days, fifteen years or one hundred years."

Perhaps the failure of Mrs. St. John's premonition is best explained by Harold Sherman, founder and president of the ESP Research Associates Foundation, who wrote that the "intervention of other forces in the interim following the prediction may change the causations and thus alter or cancel the event predicted." Whether "other forces" were at work in the case of the Niagara Falls prediction we cannot say. We can only suggest that every premonition is accompanied by this possibility of intervention. Premonitions are pointers to probability rather than omens of the immutable. Premonitions don't *have* to happen. But, unless man or nature acts to alter the momentum of events, the likelihood is that they will.

The Maids of the Mist tour boats parade in Niagara Gorge. The Falls didn't fall after all.

The Great Pyramid of Gizeh.
Its stone encases a series of
predictions about the world's
fate.

13 From the Great Pyramid to the Cheshire Idiot

Any lingering doubts the reader may have about the inordinate range of prophetic material will be dispelled with the following selections. The strangest predictions are made by the most unusual people in the weirdest of ways . . .

The Great Pyramid

The Great Pyramid of Gizeh is said to contain the prophetic word. A chronological line runs through the pyramid, indicating through the peculiarities of construction the most significant events in history, beginning from the laying of the foundation stone around 3350 B.C. The Bible bears out the pyramid's importance. Isaiah 19:19, 20 says, "In that day shall there be an altar to the Lord in the midst of the land of Egypt, and a pillar at the border thereof to the Lord. And it shall be for a sign and for a witness unto the Lord of hosts in the land of Egypt." Max Toth in his book *Pyramid Prophecies* (1979) relates the most current predictions based on the Great Pyramid:

1980-1991 . . . . The world will be turned on its side after a cataclysm alters the earth's axis; there will be major climate changes. A new spiritual influence will take hold and enlighten the world's leaders. Lands will rise and sink because of war, and disaster will be brought on by rain.

1995-2025 . . . . A new human society with a purely spiritual allegiance will be formed: "the Kingdom of the Spirit." Natural eruptions, electrical storms and other disturbances will become a way of life. Civilization will continue to decline until the turn of the century and finally collapse around 2025, after which a new society will be established.

2034	. . . . A sign of the Messiah's appearance emblazoned in the sky.
2040	. . . . The long-awaited Messiah returns incarnated in a physical body.
2055-2080	. . . . Materialistic progress reawakens with expanded growth of prosperity and achievement.
2080-2115	. . . . New spiritual expansiveness with mankind's consciousness raised to new heights.
Circa 2116	. . . . Passing of incarnated Messiah, who takes form again around 2135, and a third time around 2265.

In *Dramatic Prophecies of the Great Pyramids* (1961), Rudolfo Benavides of Mexico City speculates that a world cataclysm could occur by 1982 in conjunction with the shifting of the earth's axis. From 1982 to 1987, he expects a rise of up to sixty feet in the world's sea level as a result of melting ice-caps and sustained rainfall. Then, from 1987 to 2001, comes a catastrophic period in which up to seventy per cent of the world's population will be wiped out, leading to an era without a Jewish nation.

The Future of Canada

"No man can despair who ponders the position of the Dominion in 1983." With these words, Ralph Centennius, writing in 1883, sums up his too-good-to-be-true vision of Canada one hundred years on. In a 10,000 word essay entitled *The Dominion in 1983*, he portrays a land of social and technological perfection.

There are no taxes, murder and suicide have disappeared, sickness has been all but obliterated (each large city needs only one clinic with three doctors) and stormy weather is under man's control. "Rocket cars," traveling 500 feet above the ground, hurtle from Toronto to Vancouver Island in fifty minutes and pollution-free automobiles are propelled by "oxhydrogen charge."

Centennius foresaw 93 million Canadians (instead of the current 23 million) populating the nation all the way "to the shores of the Arctic Ocean." Rightly, he predicted Toronto and Montreal would be the largest cities. Wrongly, he foresaw chilly Churchill on Hudson Bay as a seaside resort!

On the international scene, Centennius tells us that wars in Europe have ceased and that an "Imperial Confederation" of English-speaking peoples has become a reality. Only the Russians "retain much of their old brutish disposition and ferocity in the midst of all the civilized influences of modern times."

Jules Verne

In his books *From the Earth to the Moon* (1865) and *Round the Moon* (1870), Jules Verne gave us the scenario of man exploring space. Let's compare the journey of Verne's nineteenth century astronauts with the Apollo XIII mission 100 years later, bearing in mind that Verne wrote his stories more than thirty years before the first aircraft was built:

	VERNE	NASA, March 1970
Rocket base:	Tampa, Florida	Cape Kennedy, Florida
Name of craft:	Columbiad	Columbia
Crew:	3	3
Escape velocity:	25,000 m.p.h.	24,000 m.p.h.
Travel time:	97 hr. 13 m. 20 sec.	97 hr. 39 m.
Flight calculations prepared:	Cambridge, England	Cambridge, U.S.A.
Type of food:	compressed food, "reduced by strong hydraulic pressure to the smallest possible dimensions."	dehydrated solids and concentrated liquids.
Problems:	Potential freezing and oxygen loss resulting in aborted moon landing.	Small explosion threatening loss of oxygen and freezing. Moon landing called off.
Tracking station:	Rocky Mountains	Around the world, including western U.S. mountain ranges.
Return to earth:	Splash-down in the Pacific Ocean. Recovery of floating capsule by specially modified vessel.	The same.

Jonathan Swift

In *Gulliver's Travels* (1726), English satirist Jonathan Swift predicted the two moons that revolve around Mars 151 years before they were spotted by American astronomer Asaph Hall. Today's scientists are still wondering how Gulliver's creator acquired his foresight. For not only did Swift pinpoint the existence of the two moons, naming them *Deimos* and *Phobos*, he also pointed out that one of them traveled faster than the other. All this, of course, without the aid of a telescope.

An unassuming predictor himself, Swift enjoyed nothing more than to poke fun at the astrology-mongers who were flourishing in England at the time. Using the pseudonym Isaac Bickerstaff, he went so far as to publish a volume entitled *Predictions for the Year 1708* in which he ridiculed a certain John Partridge, one of the more prosperous purveyors of astrological almanacs. "My first prediction is but a trifle," announced Bickerstaff's almanac. "Yet I will make it to show how ignorant these sottish pretenders to astrology are in their own concerns. It relates to Partridge the almanac maker. I have consulted the star of his nativity by my own rules and find he will infallibly die upon the 29th. of March next, about eleven at night, of a raging fever. Therefore I advise him to consider of it, and settle his affairs in time."

Swift must have enjoyed the joke immensely: Partridge protested vehemently while astrology addicts lapped up the hoax with the greatest conviction. Once March 29 had passed, Isaac Bickerstaff promptly put out another pamphlet inscribed, *An account of the death of Mr. Partridge, the Almanac maker, upon the 29th Instant, in a letter from a Revenue Officer to a Person of Honour.* The unfortunate Partridge, who became the butt of a number of practical jokes, was obliged to advertize that he was still alive. For a while, however, Partridge was officially dead, and even the Stationers' Hall was fooled into solemnly removing his name from their rolls!

The Visions at Fatima

The Roman Catholic world still trembles from the prophetic visions seen by three shepherd children near the Portuguese village of Fatima during the First World War. On May 13, 1917, Lucia, 10, Francisco, 9, and Giacinta, 7, were tending sheep on a high ridge of land called the Cova da Iria when they looked up to see "a beautiful lady from heaven" who talked to them for several minutes. The apparition promised to return, and indeed reappeared on the thirteenth of every month until October.

As word of the vision spread, the numbers of people accompanying the children to the Cova da Iria grew. By October 13, more than 50,000 flocked in pouring rain to the sacred spot. This time, the shining figure in the sky identified herself as Our Lady Of The Rosary and offered, for the children's ears only, three messages of forthcoming events. Although the huge crowd could neither hear nor see the apparition, they all witnessed a strange series of events. The rain suddenly stopped, the clouds dispersed and the sun appeared in a blue sky. Eye-witnesses, including journalists and skeptics as well as Christian devotees, swore the sun wobbled, spun then plunged toward earth, radiating long fingers of light that cast colored shadows across the landscape. Three times this phenomenon was repeated as the terrified onlookers fell to their knees and prayed.

Though Francisco and Giacinta died of influenza before 1920, Lucia later wrote down the three secrets of Fatima. In the first message, she revealed how the Virgin had shown her a sea of fire in which demons and "beings in human form, charred and black, like hot coals" were carried skyward by flames where they were reduced to sparks "without weight or equilibrium, emitting loud cries and screams of pain and desperation." The second message foreshadowed World War Two and the emerging might of Russia. Lucia quoted the "beautiful lady" as saying:

> The war [1914-18] is coming to an end. But if people do not cease to offend the Lord, another and more terrible one will break out during the next pontificate. When you see the night lit up by a great, unknown light, know that it is a sign that God gives you that punishment of the world by another war, famine and persecution of the Church and of the Holy Father.
>
> In order to prevent this, I have come to intercede for the conversion of Russia . . . If you carry out my requests, Russia will be converted and there will be peace. If not, Russia will extend her errors throughout the world, provoking wars and persecutions against the Church. Many good people will become martyrs. The Holy Father will suffer much. Several nations will be annihilated.
>
> In the end, however, my Immaculate Heart will triumph; Russia will be converted and the world will enjoy a period of peace.

The first part of this prophecy was fulfilled between 9 and 11 p.m. on the night of January 25, 1938, when a crimson glow illuminated the skies of western Europe. In the Alps, it was so brilliant that night postal employees worked without artificial light. One newspaper ran

the headline: AURORA BOREALIS STARTLES EUROPE: PEO-
PLE FLEE IN FEAR, and reported that the lights "spread fear in
parts of Portugal, while thousands of Britons were brought running
into the streets in wonderment."

Lucia, who became a nun in Coimbra, Portugal, had been instructed in a subsequent vision not to reveal the last message until
1960. But the world still awaits the official version of this final
prediction. For after the message was opened in Portugal in 1960
and forwarded to the Pope, its contents never got any further than
the Vatican. Pope John XXIII was later said to have "trembled with
fear and almost fainted with horror" at what he read. An unauth-
enticated text purporting to be the mysterious third message was,
however, published in Germany on October 15, 1963. An extract
from the prophecy according to *News Europa* reads:

> A great war will break out in the second half of the twentieth
> century. Fire and smoke will fall from heaven, the waters of
> the oceans will become vapors, the scum will arise in a confused
> manner, and everything will sink down. Millions and millions
> of men will perish while this is going on and those who survive
> will envy the dead. The unexpected will follow in every part
> of the world, anxiety, pain and misery in every country. Have
> I seen it? The time is getting ever nearer and the abyss is getting
> wider without hope. The good will perish with the bad, the

The last pope surrounded by
adversaries—a vision of the
end of the papacy
according to Paracelsus.

great with the small, the heads of the Church with their faithful, and the rulers with their people. There will be death everywhere as a result of the mistakes of the unfeeling and the partisans of Satan, but when those who survive all these happenings are still alive, they will proclaim God again and His glory, and will serve him as in the time when the world was not so perverted.

Paracelsus

Just as Swiss cheese is full of holes, so are the predictions of the Swiss prophet Paracelsus (1493-1541) riddled with imperspicuity. His profoundly mystical prophecies consist of thirty-two allegorical pictures, each accompanied by an explanation. Not that the explanations make Theophrastus Bombast Von Hohenheim Paracelsus (his full name) any easier to understand. In fact, many of his picture symbols make the obscure quatrains of Nostradamus appear positively lucid in comparison. The Seventh Figure, one of the few drawings that can be interpreted, shows a robed churchman standing in a river, surrounded by spears. Apparently, Paracelsus was predicting the downfall of the papacy. The inscription reads:

Paracelsus: predictions riddled with imperspicuity.

> Because from time to time thou hast been self-willed, thou art predestined to be surrounded by much adversity. For thou hast not considered of thyself how thou art prefigured magically under the symbol of a stone, as both fat and lean. Thou dost not know it, therefore thou fallest beneath the punishment that hath broken up all empires. Had thy pretended wisdom and understanding been thine own, thou wouldst have been beyond disaster, and moreover, other empires would have taken thee as a mirror. But it is not so, therefore thy wisdom proveth to be a folly at this time.

In another prophecy, Paracelsus warns the "northern countries" of frightful consequences following the "great and fearful eclipse of the sun":

> I say that then there shall overflow as the waters of a mighty river all kinds of revolts, riots, wars, slaughter, murders, conflagrations and all evil into the northern countries.
> Then beware Brabant, Flanders and Zeeland and ye who, like my Swiss countrymen, feed upon cheese.
> Then will the Lily be altogether decayed, exhausted and cast down.

In the same wise will the Eagle be plucked, dishonored, insulted and despised.

Paracelsus said he wrote the prophecies because "it is time to show men their madness," although he admitted his symbols were "intelligible but to a small number of the elect." A revolutionary spirit as well as a brilliant physician and alchemist who was to be revered by historians as the first great medical scientist, Paracelsus was unequivocal about at least one thing: he accurately predicted the time and place of his death in Salzburg, Austria.

Count Hamon

Count Louis Hamon, otherwise known as Cheiro, was an English gentleman with impeccable credentials as a predictor. He forecast the Boer War, the time of Queen Victoria's death, the assassination of King Umberto of Italy, the First World War and the Great Depression of the thirties. He said that King Edward VII would live to the age of 69; Edward, born in 1841, died in 1910 after ruling England for nine years. Hamon anticipated the "devastating love affair" and subsequent abdication of King Edward VIII and told Mark Twain, when Twain was broke, that he would be a rich man in 1903. In 1902, Twain signed a contract guaranteeing him $25,000 a year from his books. By 1903, he had earned $60,000 in royalties.

Cheiro (1866-1936) foresaw women gaining more and more responsibility in world affairs. "Women," he said, "have to come to the front in all matters of public life. I have no hesitation in saying that there is no body of men who will be able for long to resist the tide of thought that, for good or evil, is bringing women into power."

The Count also said that communism "will spread like an infective fever through all the countries" and he sided with Biblical prophecy about Armageddon. "It is only war in the end that will save humanity," he declared. "It is only when the world will be satiated with blood, destruction and violence that it will wake from its present nightmare of madness — and thus it is that the coming 'War of Wars' fits into the design of things."

Mother Shipton

Poor old Mother Shipton. The sixteenth century Yorkshire crone with the horribly bulbous nose may well have nurtured a rare prophetic talent, but so many forgers have abused her name that today it's impossible to separate the genuine prophecies from the fakes.

Though Mother Shipton supposedly scored with a number of predictions, including Sir Walter Raleigh's discovery of tobacco and the potato, Drake's defeat of the Spanish Armada and the finding of gold in Australia — long before Australia itself was discovered — she's remembered most of all for predicting the car, telegraph, railway, submarine, airplane and the end of the world in 1881. In 1862, however, English editor and hoaxer-in-chief Charles Hindley confessed he'd penned the lines on which her reputation rests:

Mother Shipton: Hoaxers have hopped onto her broomstick and used her name to further their own fortunes.

Carriages without horses shall go
And accidents fill the world with woe,
Around the earth thoughts shall fly,
In the twinkling of an eye.

Through the hills man shall ride,
And no horse be at his side.
Under water men shall walk,
Shall ride, shall sleep, shall walk,
In the air men shall be seen,
In white in black in green.
Iron in the water shall float
As easily as a wooden boat.

Fire and water shall wonders do
England shall at last admit a foe
The world to an end shall come
In eighteen hundred and eighty-one.

Forgery though it is, this passage proved to be remarkably accurate; Hindley *was* ahead of his time. But many people still believed Mother Shipton was its real source, and when 1881 rolled around, they prepared to leave their homes and possessions to ready themselves for the last trump.

Mother Shipton died in 1561, some eighty years before her first prophecies came to light. Very accurate up to the publication date, they proved to be not so impressive afterward. Whatever the truth of her prophesying, the "devil's child," as Mother Shipton was called by her neighbors, was quite a figure in her time. When Cardinal Wolsey dispatched his aides to make her recant her prediction of his downfall, she demonstrated her powers by throwing a linen handkerchief into her fire, cackling wickedly when it refused to burn. For some years up until 1839, her wax effigy stood in Westminster Abbey alongside such notables as Queen Elizabeth and Oliver Cromwell.

Merlin the Predictor

Merlin, the most legendary of British prophets, spoke knowledgeably of events centuries ahead of his time. Way back in the fifth century he foretold the nickname, the career and the death of the crusading Richard I (1157-1199):

The Lionheart will 'gainst the Saracen rise,
And purchase from him many a glorious prize . . .
Coop'ed up and cag'd the Lion then shall be,
But after suffrance ransom'ed and set free,
. . . Last by a poisonous shaft, the Lion die.

Merlin predicted the Gunpowder Plot of 1605. He told of "wolves" undermining the Crown and government by

Striving in Hell to register their names,
By blowing up the State in powder flames.

Foreseeing his own people, the Welsh, surrendering their autonomy, he wrote:

You will keep your language and your race, but of your old kingdom, nothing will remain but Gwalia's rugged mountains.

And he said the time would come in England when

. . . parents shall be hated by their children, men of worship shall have no reverence of their inferiours; chastitie shall be broken with maidens, wives and widows, religious men and virgins, with more ill than I can tell of, from the which God us defend.

The Fire of London

The prophet William Lilly was awarded the highest tribute of a skeptical establishment when hauled before a Parliamentary Committee in 1666. Lilly's prediction of the great plague and fire of London (1665-6) was so accurate that, once the fire had died down, the committee wanted to investigate him. It was suspected he'd either been bribed by a foreign power to commit arson or that he'd set the blaze on his own initiative to fulfill his prophecy. Finding nothing to incriminate Lilly, however, the investigators allowed him to go free. Here, committed to paper in 1648, is what got their suspicious minds working:

In the year 1665 . . . so grand a catastrophe and great mutation . . . will be ominous to London, unto her merchants at sea, to her traffique on land, to her poor, to all sorts of people, inhabiting in her or to her liberties, by reason of sundry fires and a consuming plague.

Lilly wasn't the only Londoner to predict the fire. Seer Humphrey Smith said that his fiery vision in 1660 "remained in me as a thing secretly shewed me of the Lord." And George Fox, founder of the Society of Friends, told how a man called Thomas Ibbott, arriving in London two days before the blaze, leapt from his horse and ran through the streets shouting that he was fleeing from the flames. Those who stood and laughed were imitating his antics within forty-eight hours.

The Vicissitudes of John Dee

The see-saw career of astrologer John Dee (1527-1608) went up and down according to who sat on the English throne. At first, he languished in prison on a charge of using enchantments against Queen Mary after making this prediction about her upcoming Spanish marriage:

> Woe to the two nations: woe and sorrow
> Disaster by water: persecution by fire
> And the Queen shall childless die.

That's the way it turned out. Mary, who died childless, entangled the nation in a war of alliance with Spain that depleted England's sea power. At home, Protestants were ruthlessly persecuted, and many of them were burnt at the stake. Unpleasant though this prophecy was, nothing could be proved against Dee, and he was freed from jail by order of the Privy Council.

When Elizabeth became queen she encouraged Dee's career — quite possibly because he had predicted her accession. He was asked to choose a good day for the coronation and favored with the job of court astrologer. He savored the success of forecasting the execution of Mary Queen of Scots in 1587, four years before it happened, and his advice is said to have influenced the time Sir Francis Drake set sail to rout the Spanish Armada.

But when James was made king in 1603, John Dee found himself back in the doghouse. James' expert on witchcraft denounced the astrologer as an "ally of Satan" and he was forced to forfeit his position at court. Dee kicked up a fuss, inviting his accusers to try him publicly as a witch. But his challenge was not accepted and Dee was simply ignored. Five years later he died, a disillusioned and peacefully retired old man.

Worlds in Collision

Galactic scientist Immanuel Velikovsky pored over ancient religious and mythological texts to fashion his predictions that shocked the scientific world. Finding accounts of great cataclysms recurring in the lore of different cultures, he decided to accept the legends as truth rather than fable. He speculated in *Worlds In Collision* (1974) that changes in the configuration of the planets (Venus and Mars wobbling in orbit, for example) had caused a series of great upheavals on Earth. As recently as 2000 B.C., says Russian-born Velikovsky, the earth shifted its rotational axis and reversed its poles; day suddenly became night and tropical and arctic zones exchanged

Immanuel Velikovsky fashioned predictions out of fable.

climates. Continents tilted and tidal waves and hurricanes swept the globe. Velikovsky maintains some cataclysms struck with such violence and speed that animals and plants were frozen instantly, an idea that counters conventional science's belief that well-preserved mammoths found in Siberia died naturally before being buried under slowly advancing ice.

Spurned as "rubbish and nonsense" by some astronomers and scientists, Velikovsky's theories either alienate or enthrall his readers. His earth-in-upheaval speculations have yet to be confirmed, but the following predictions have been proven by scientific investigation:

- Venus has an atmosphere of hydrocarbons and a surface temperature of about 1,000 degrees F. that's quickly cooling. (Space probes have since found evidence of a hydrocarbon atmosphere and have determined that the planet's surface heat is slightly less than 1,000° F. and dropping rapidly.)
- The earth is surrounded by a magnetosphere. (The discovery in the mid-fifties of the Van Allen Belt of magnetic particles around the earth proved this, although the field grows weaker away from the earth, not stronger as Velikovsky suggested.)
- The last ice age occurred three times more recently than has been conventionally assumed. (In 1952, radiocarbon studies of fossils forced a revision of existing glacial theories.)
- The soil of the moon contains hydrocarbons and dried molten lava only a few thousand years old. (This was confirmed by analysis of moon rock samples.)

Predictors at War

As World War Two raged across Europe, a shadowy war of prediction was being fought by astrologers employed by the opposing sides. Advising Hitler was Karl Ernst Krafft who, as well as charting what the stars signified for the Nazi regime, selected and angled the prophecies of Nostradamus to forecast the inevitability of a German victory with the aim of demoralizing the people of occupied France. Meanwhile, in London, Louis de Wohl backed Churchill by anticipating and countering what the Nazi predictors were up to. De Wohl wrote in 1952 that it was his task to come "to the same interpretative results" as the enemy forecasters, but to turn them in favor of England. While de Wohl survived the war, Krafft was not so fortunate. Although he accurately predicted Hitler would be in danger during the first ten days of November, 1939 (during this time, a bomb explosion ripped through a Munich beer cellar shortly after Hitler had left), Krafft was not exempted from a state crackdown on astrologers and other occultists in 1941. At first imprisoned in Berlin, he later died in Buchenwald concentration camp on January 8, 1945.

Not even her arrest by the Gestapo prevented Elise Lehrer from predicting the downfall of Nazi Germany. Repeating her prophecy for as long as she was able, Miss Lehrer died in Ravensbruck concentration camp before she could savor the truth of her words. Earlier, she foretold the fire that destroyed priceless works of art in the Munich Palace of Glass. And before that, she refused to join friends on an excursion because she foresaw a train accident. She persuaded two of them to stay home, but two others left as planned and were killed when the train crashed.

Tribal Suicide

Twenty-five thousand South African natives starved to death in 1857 — because they believed a prediction of everlasting plenty.

The prophet Umhlakaza, passing on a message received in a trance by his niece Nongquase, told his people the spirits of dead chiefs had commanded that everything edible, including cattle, must be eaten or destroyed. Then on February 18, 1857, a blood-red sun would rise and a great hurricane would drive all white men and unbelieving natives into the sea. Fields of ripe grain and herds of magnificent cattle would miraculously appear.

In vain, the colonial government of British Kaffraria tried to prevent the ensuing destruction. Cattle were slaughtered, grain-bins emptied and crops laid waste. When the great day dawned without the promised miracle, the disillusionment was as deep as the anticipation had been feverish. The natives' despair was matched only by their hunger. As the famine took hold, many squatted in groups and waited to die, some trekked to neighboring areas to work or beg for food and others turned in desperation to cannibalism.

Doctor Jung

Swiss psychologist Carl Jung had premonitions of the First World War. He first felt a sense of oppression in the autumnn of 1913 and later, while on a journey, was "suddenly seized with an overpowering vision: I saw a monstrous flood covering all the northern and low-lying lands between the North Sea and the Alps. When it came up to Switzerland I saw that the mountains grew higher and higher to protect our country. I realized that a frightful catastrophe was in progress. I saw the mighty yellow waves, the floating rubble of civilization, and the drowned bodies of uncounted thousands. Then the whole sea turned to blood." The vision which lasted about an hour left Jung feeling "perplexed and nauseated, and ashamed of my weakness."

Two weeks later the vision returned, this time accompanied by a voice that told him, "Look at it well; it is wholly real . . ." Next, in the spring and summer of 1914, he had dreams of an Arctic cold gripping the world. Jung was starting to wonder if he was losing his hold on reality when the war broke out, convincing him his experiences were prophetic rather than psychotic.

The Eternal Feminine

Russian seer Nicholas Berdyaev saw the world heading for what he called the "new Middle Ages." In *The End of Our Time* (1923), he anticipates the rejection of materialism and the blossoming of womanhood into "the eternal feminine." Nevertheless, our lives will be fraught with danger as we "leave the rational day to enter the dark night of the Middle Ages." Berdyaev wrote:

> The notion of "progress" will be discarded as camouflaging the true ends of life, there will be creation, there will be turning to God or to Satan . . . Women will be very much to the fore in the new Middle Ages . . . This extended activity of women in the future does not at all mean a development of that "women's emancipation" with which we are familiar, the end and method of which is to reduce woman to the likeness of man by leading her along a masculine road . . . It is the *eternal feminine* that has so great a future in coming history, not the emancipated woman.

A Step Ahead of the Rockets

Three times precognition saved Cyril Macklin from being killed at work during the Second World War.

The first escape was made from a London factory canteen after he suddenly felt sick and was plagued by a buzzing in his ears.

Macklin, who'd earlier predicted the outbreak of hostilities and even named the London streets that would be destroyed, became so upset that he handed in his notice and left the building. Minutes later, the canteen was flattened by German bombers.

Escape number two followed another bout of nausea, this time in his new factory job in Acton. He was conducting an air raid shelter drill when he "saw" an unexploded bomb bounce through the shelter's open door and smash into a woman's legs. Again he quit his job, later to hear that his premonition had come true.

Relocated at a Wimbledon factory, Macklin was about to show up for a night shift when an inner voice cautioned, "Don't go tonight." Not being one to argue with his psychic intuition, he stayed home. Hours later, his workshop was leveled in yet another raid.

Hepatoscopy

As far as we know, the future was first foretold in ancient Babylon by means of hepatoscopy — the dubious science of examining animals' livers. The Babylonians, or Chaldeans, as they were called, regarded the liver as the seat of life. Novice soothsayers were trained with the help of clay models marked with the liver's signs of portent, such as the organ's general shape and condition and the color and quality of the blood. Hepatoscopy was confined to the ruling class. Only the king and his nobles were allowed to participate in the solemn ceremony of killing the animal, extracting its liver and placing it reverently upon an altar.

The Chaldeans abandoned this gory practice hundreds of years before the birth of Christ to pioneer the refinements of astrological prediction, but the Romans carried on where they left off. Their haruspices, or liver-readers, were always Etruscan by birth, since the Romans were loath to commit themselves about anything. These prophets had their own college in Rome and generally confined themselves to examining the heart or liver of an ox. The animal had to be without blemish and still alive when the organ was hacked from its body. Whoever was accepting the reading always prayed for deliverance from the worst possible omen: a shriveled, dried-up liver.

The China Syndrome

The U.S. Atomic Energy Commission anticipated the possibility of a potentially lethal nuclear accident by starting work on a $500 million "loss of fluid test facility" in the Idaho wilderness in 1969. Five theoretical tests were later made of back-up systems in the event of nuclear fuel being deprived of cooling water. And in December, 1978, a test was conducted involving "live" nuclear fuel. The test pointed to the systems' safety.

But on March 28, 1979, safeguards at the nuclear power plant on Three Mile Island in central Pennsylvania failed after the facility's fuel suffered a loss of cooling water. Radioactive steam drifted across the countryside and the radiation-proof containment building was flooded with 650,000 gallons of radioactive water. Another 65,000 gallons escaped through a drain into an adjoining building which was not radiation-tight.

The nuclear test site in the Idaho wilderness.

The China Syndrome — a film predicting the problems, dangers and moral dilemmas encountered on Three Mile Island — was released just before the accident happened. And in August, 1979, James Creswell, a reactor inspector for the Nuclear Regulatory Commission, told the President's panel investigating the accident that he had warned his bosses about the dangers of a mishap like the one at Three Mile Island. But his efforts led only to a bad performance report.

The Cheshire Idiot

Robert Nixon was a plowboy who lived in Cheshire in the fifteenth century. He was also an ugly, surly, gluttonous, grunting, slavering fool. Sometimes, however, his crippling handicaps were mysteriously suspended, and he spoke with great lucidity and accuracy about the future. He foretold the English Civil War, the French Revolution and many of the dramatic events that were to mark the history of the English monarchy. Henry VII, impressed by tales of the prophetic powers of the "Cheshire Idiot," summoned him to his court. But Robert, having predicted the summons and his death by starvation if he obeyed, refused to go until a military escort knocked on his door. He ended up living with the kitchen staff and so annoyed the royal retinue with constant demands for food that, when the king was away hunting, he was locked in an empty room for his own protection. Too late was his confinement remembered, and by the time the room was unlocked, the Cheshire Idiot had starved to death. Of his prophecies still waiting to be fulfilled are two that suggest war between England and Russia:

Through our own money and our men,
Shall a dreadful war begin.
Between the sickle and the suck
All England shall have a pluck.

And:

Foreign nations shall invade England
with snow on their helmets, and shall
bring plague, famine and murder in
the skirts of their garments.

The Last Word

"The future can be seen, and because it can be seen, it can be changed."

J. B. Priestley

So what do we do? Can we turn the world around, or do we move to one of Cayce's "safety lands" as far as possible from the armed camps of world power?

If Priestley is to be believed, there's hope yet — but not in running away. Predictions tell us life is going to get a lot worse before it gets a lot better. Predictions point to our miserable end should we heedlessly tread the paths that history has shown lead only to disaster. But — and this is the clincher — what actually transpires is always what we choose. If we care enough to change our ways, we can make nonsense of the predictors' gloomiest pronouncements.

It's not enough to fear the worst and hope for the best — it's what we *do* that counts. Whether the year 2000 is rung in with merrymaking or whether it steals upon a world preoccupied with killing and dying is up to us. Predictions only help those who help themselves.

Prediction Timetable

Predictions don't arrive with the regularity of commuter trains. Some come from the distant past; others are but half uttered. Although every effort has been made to supply complete information, a few gaps are inevitable, considering the far-flung sources of many of these predictions. Where the predictor has specified no date, or where the prediction is general enough to cover the entire world, but no one place more than another, we've left the entry blank. It will be up to future generations to fill in these blanks.

TYPE OF PREDICTION	WHO OR WHAT IT WAS ABOUT	PREDICTOR AND DATE	WHEN IT WAS PREDICTED TO HAPPEN	WHEN IT ACTUALLY HAPPENED	PAGE
Geophysical					
Atlantis	Discovery of remains at Bimini	Edgar Cayce, 1940	1968-69	1968	82
comet	Comet strikes Earth	Jeane Dixon, 1978	1985		94
earth upheaval	Worldwide upheaval	Nostradamus, 1555	May 10, ?		55
	US coasts	Edgar Cayce, 1934	1998		76
	Alaska earthquake	Jeane Dixon, 1964	1964	1964	90
	US and Europe	Gribben & Plagemann, 1974	1982		80
	China earthquake	Kathy Sotka, 1976	1976	1976	106
	Worldwide upheaval	Ross Peterson, 1977	1989-2030		105
	World reshaped	Jeane Dixon, 1978	2000		94
	California hit	Ernesto Montgomery, 1978	1983		101
	US affected	Irene Hughes, 1979	1981-82, 1986		102
floods	Ireland	St. Columbcille, 565 A.D.			36
	New York	Nostradamus, 1555			55
	Japan	Edgar Cayce, 1941	1998		76
	Worldwide	Jeane Dixon, 1964	2000		94
	Australia	John Nash, 1975	1976		173
ice age	Worldwide effects	Immanuel Velikovsky, 1947	1952		201
	Worldwide effects	Irene Hughes, 1979	1983-1989		102
meteor	London disaster	Criswell, 1978	1988		106
Political					
assassination	Julius Caesar	Spurinna, 44 B.C.	March 15, 44 B.C.	March 15, 44 B.C.	66
	Richard I	Merlin, 5th century A.D.		1199	198
	MacBeth	Three witches, 1054	1054	1054	62
	British Prime Minister Perceval	John Williams, May, 1812	May, 1812	May, 1812	185
	Foresaw his own assassination	Abraham Lincoln, April 8, 1865	near future	April 11, 1865	185
	Foresaw his own assassination	Rasputin, December, 1916	near future	January 1, 1917	34
	John F. Kennedy	Jeane Dixon, 1952		November 22, 1963	92
	Robert Kennedy	Jeane Dixon, May 28, 1968	near future	June 4, 1968	93
	The Pope assassinated	Irene Hughes, 1979			102
change of power or influence	Alexander the Great's defeat	Book of Daniel, 3rd century B.C.		323 B.C.	18
	Indonesia's independence	Prince Jayabhaya, 12th century A.D.		1950	36
	Haile Selassie crowned	Marcus Garvey, 1920s		1930	50
	Churchill's defeat	Jeane Dixon, 1945	near future	1945	90
	Partition of India	Jeane Dixon, 1946	near future	1947	90
	Nixon's election	Jeane Dixon, 1949	near future	1968	97
	Algeria's uprising	Bertrand de Jouvenel, 1951	near future	1954	158
	Canada and Brazil gain power through food resources	Jean Dixon, 1978	2000		95
	Australia, Canada, New Zealand unite	Jeane Dixon, 1979	1990s		95
end of monarchy	Gunpowder Plot	Merlin, 5th Century A.D.		1605	199
	End of Dalai Lama's rule	Tibetan prediction, circa 1400		1959	90
	Cortes invades Mexico	Montezuma, 1508		1519	32

Category	Event	Source	Predicted	Actual	Page
	Mary Queen of Scots executed	John Dee, 1583	near future	1587	200
	Emperor Matthias dies	Johannes Kepler, 1610	near future	1619	184
	Shah of Iran deposed	Hudson Institute, 1978		1979	159
	Queen Elizabeth abdicates	Irene Hughes, 1979			102
nations oppressed	Take-over of Wales	Merlin, 5th century A.D.		1409	199
	The Irish Rebellion	St. Columbille, 565 A.D.		1641	34
new nations arising	Creation of Israel	Book of Ezekiel, 6th century B.C.		1948	21
	Creation of Israel	Edgar Cayce, 1933	near future	1948	76
	Quebec secedes from Canada	Irene Hughes, 1979	1985		102
nuclear destruction	Middle East	Book of Zechariah, 6th century B.C.			25
	Scotland	Brahan Seer, 1665			60
	Worldwide	Robert Silverberg, 1973			141
peace	After nuclear war	Book of Micah, 8th century B.C.			26
	Worldwide	Nostradamus, 1555			56
	Peace in Northern Ireland	Jeane Dixon, 1979	1988		95
terrorism	International nuclear blackmail	H. G. Wells, 1895	near future		156
	Worldwide terrorism	Yehezkel Dror, mid-1970s	near future		156
	Worldwide terrorism	Rand Corporation, 1974	near future		156
	Stolen nuclear weapon	Jeane Dixon, 1979	1981		94
totalitarian mind control	In *The Iron Heel*	Jack London, 1907	near future		133
	In *We*	Eugene Zamiatin, 1920	near future		133
	In *Brave New World*	Aldous Huxley, 1931	2531		138
	In *1984*	George Orwell, 1947	1984		129
	In *Fahrenheit 451*	Ray Bradbury, 1953	near future		137
WAR: World War I	Dreams pointing to World War I	Carl Jung, 1913	near future	1914	203
World War II	Hitler and the invasion of Eastern Europe	Nostradamus, 1555		1941	48
	World War	Brahan Seer, 1665		1939	66
	World War	The Fatima predictions, 1919	near future	1939	193
	Worldwide conflict	Edgar Cayce, 1936	near future	1939	82
	End of war in Europe	Basil Shackleton, 1940	August 17, 1945	May 7, 1945	105
	Hitler's downfall	Elise Lehrer, 1941	near future	1945	203
Armageddon	Middle East	Book of Ezekiel, 6th century B.C.			22
	Worldwide	Nostradamus, 1555			54
	Worldwide	Brahan Seer, 1665			66
	Worldwide	The Fatima predictions, 1919	before 2000		194
	Disarmament broken	Jeane Dixon, 1978	1999		94
	Worldwide	Gopi Krishna, 1979	near future		107
	War in Africa	Simon Alexander, 1979	2000		103
	War in Africa	Jeane Dixon, 1979	1987		95
	Third Indochina war	Jeane Dixon, 1979	1985		95
West vs. East	China unleashes germ warfare	Jeane Dixon, 1978	1980s		94
	China vs. Russia	Jeane Dixon, 1978	2020-2037		94
	China vs. USA	Irene Hughes, 1979	1980s		102
women in power	First woman American president	Jeane Dixon, 1978	1980s		95
	World government led by a woman	Ann Jensen, 1978	1991-2000		107

Social

TYPE OF PREDICTION	WHO OR WHAT IT WAS ABOUT	PREDICTOR AND DATE	WHEN IT WAS PREDICTED TO HAPPEN	WHEN IT ACTUALLY HAPPENED	PAGE
cities destroyed	Great fire and plague of London	William Lilly, 1648	1665	1665-1666	199
	Paris	Nostradamus, 1555	1998		55
	New York, Los Angeles, San Francisco	Edgar Cayce, 1934	2006		76
	New York, Los Angeles	Ross Peterson, 1977	2006		105
	Rome and Paris	Irene Hughes, 1979	2000		102
cities, domed	Manhattan covered to save heat	Buckminster Fuller, 1969	near future		124
cities established	Earth capital in Alaska	David Hoy, 1979	2029		107
cities evacuated	North America	Adam Cuthand, 1979	1995		132
cities, floating	US off-shore	Buckminster Fuller, 1969	near future		124
cities in space	Located in the asteroid belt	Freeman Dyson, 1970	2000		153
	Orbiting the earth	Gerard O'Neill, 1975	2150		152
	Located in near space	F. M. Esfandiary, 1978	2000		157
megalopolises	New York, the "new city"	Nostradamus, 1555	2800		55
	Cities of millions in US and Europe	Jules Verne, 1875	after 2000		122
	Worldwide urban sprawl	Oswald Spengler, died 1936	2000		137
	US urban centers, such as *Boswash*	Herman Kahn, 1979			149
destruction of nuclear family	Becomes a commercial unit	Karl Marx, 1883	near future		133
	In *Brave New World*	Aldous Huxley, 1931	2531		139
	In *1984*	George Orwell, 1947	1984		134
	In *Fahrenheit 451*	Ray Bradbury, 1953	near future		138
disaster premonitions	French Revolution executions	Jacques Cazotte, 1788	near future	1789-1794	45
	Titanic sinks	W. T. Stead, 1888		1912	180
	Titanic sinks	Morgan Robertson, 1898		1912	179
	Stead perishes on the *Titanic*	Louis Hamon, 1911		1912	180
	Titanic sinks	Mrs. Marshall, April 10, 1912		April 15, 1912	181
	Death of 3 Apollo astronauts	Jeane Dixon, 1966		1967	88
	Aberfan landslide	Eryl Mai Jones, October 7, 1966		October 21, 1966	181
	Rocky Marciano's death	Thomas Casas, May, 1969		August, 1969	183
	Transportation disasters	Joseph DeLouise, 1978		1978	107
	Chicago DC-10 crash	David Booth, May, 1979		June, 1979	177
economy, rising	Western world	Daniel Bell, 1967	2000		158
	Japan	Herman Kahn, 1974	2000		149
	Worldwide	Herman Kahn, 1974	2100		148
economy, stagnating or falling	Depression cycles	Edgar Cayce, 1931	cyclical	1929, 1954, 1978	80
	Worldwide downfall of economy	The Club of Rome, 1972	2072		156
food supply, enough	Famine obliterated	Herman Kahn, 1975	near future		148
	Famine obliterated	Jeane Dixon, 1979	2000		95
food supply, new food sources	Western world	Daniel Bell, 1967	2000		158
	Ocean farming	Kathy Sotka, 1978	1986		106
food supply, too little	Ancient Egypt	Joseph, 16th century B.C.	near future		18
	Irish potato famine	St. Columbcille, 565 A.D.		1844-1850	34
	Worldwide	George Orwell, 1947	1984		130
	Famine in the US	Herbert Armstrong, 1957	1972		172
	New Yorkers feed off "weed crumbs"	Harry Harrison, 1966	1999		141
	Worldwide famine	The Club of Rome, 1972	2072		156

Topic	Prediction	Source	Predicted date	Actual date	Page
leisure-time increase	Western world will enjoy increased leisure	Daniel Bell, 1967	2000		158
papacy	The popes predicted until the last one	St. Malachy, 1140	1140-2000		36
	Pope Sixtus V	Nostradamus, 1540s		1585	42
	Papacy ends	Paracelsus, died 1541	near future		195
	Pope assassinated	Irene Hughes, 1979	near future		102
population, control	Population control through contraception	Condorcet, 1793			132
	Sexual desire turned to aggression	George Orwell, 1947	1984		139
	Effective worldwide population control	Herman Kahn, 1979	2000		148
population, decrease	Irish emigration	St. Columbcille, 565 A.D.		1845-1850	34
	Highland clearances	Brahan Seer, 1665		1747	66
	Worldwide population drop-off	Gerard O'Neill, 1975	2150		152
	Worldwide population drop-off	F. M. Esfandiary, 1978	2000		157
population, increase	Uncontrolled growth	Aldous Huxley, 1958	2531		139
	Over-population and over-consumption	Harry Harrison, 1966	1999		141
	Over-population causes a world crisis	The Club of Rome, 1972	2072		156
records kept on individuals	"Big Brother" watching over citizenry	George Orwell, 1947	1984		129
	Worldwide	Isaac Asimov, 1972	near future		126
	Data system in the US	Herman Kahn, 1979	2000		149
riots	"The leveling," e.g. the riots after King's death	Edgar Cayce, 1938	1960s	1968	82
	Food riots in New York	Harry Harrison, 1966	1999		141
trends in religion	Advertising for church-goers	H. G. Wells, 1899	near future	1950s	121
	A new religion arises	Alan Vaughan, 1973	1990s		107
	Roman Catholic church split	Jeane Dixon, 1978	1988		94
	New revelations about Jesus	Daniel Logan, 1978	1983-1987		107
	The Church declines	Simon Alexander, 1979	2000		104
universal language	Worldwide use of one language	F. M. Esfandiary, 1978			158

Space

Topic	Prediction	Source	Predicted date	Actual date	Page
astronomical discoveries	Moons of Mars discovered	Jonathan Swift, 1726		1877	191
communications satellite	Comsat satellite	Arthur C. Clarke, 1945		1975	124
Mars landing	Men walk on Mars	Frederick Davies, 1978	1983-1985		107
navigational satellite	Comsat satellite	Edward Hale, 1870		1975	120
solar energy	Near space colonies	Gerard O'Neill, 1975	1990		152
	Near space industries	Jesco von Puttkamer, 1979	near future		154
space colonies	100 leagues from Earth	Nostradamus, 1555			52
	Orbiting in near space	Arthur C. Clarke, 1958	1990		126
	Worldwide participation	Daniel Bell, 1967	2000		158
	Orbiting in near space	Isaac Asimov, 1972	2300		126
	Experimental space colony	Sandra McNeil, 1978	1990s		105
space factories	Asteroid belt	Freeman Dyson, 1970	1990		153
	Island I	Gerard O'Neill, 1975	1990		152
	Earth orbit	Richard Hiscocks, 1976	near future		154
	In the solar system	F. M. Esfandiary, 1978	2000		157
	Earth orbit	Jesco von Puttkamer, 1979	near future		154
space mining	In near space	Arthur C. Clarke, 1958	1990		126
	At "L-5"	Gerard O'Neill, 1975	2150		152
space travel	Rocket to the moon	Johannes Kepler, 1634		1959	118
	US men on the moon	Cyrano de Bergerac, 1657		1969	118
	US men on the moon	Jules Verne, 1870		1969	118
	US men on the moon	H. G. Wells, 1901		1969	118
	Sputnik I	Jeane Dixon, 1953		1957	88

TYPE OF PREDICTION	WHO OR WHAT IT WAS ABOUT	PREDICTOR AND DATE	WHEN IT WAS PREDICTED TO HAPPEN	WHEN IT ACTUALLY HAPPENED	PAGE
Technology					
air conditioning	Empire State Building first air conditioned skyscraper	Jules Verne, 1875		1931	122
aircraft	First flight at Kitty Hawk	Roger Bacon, died 1292		1903	113
	Flight of the Lilienthal Glider	Leonardo da Vinci, died 1519		1896	116
	First massive use of air warfare	Nostradamus, 1555		1940s	50
	Growth of popular aircraft	Francis Bacon, died 1626		1920s	118
	First widespread use of freighter aircraft	Alfred Lord Tennyson, 1842		1940s	52
	First flight over water by Blériot	Andrew Jackson Davis, 1856		1909	122
	Wright considers flight "unpractical"	Wilbur Wright, 1901		1903	124
airspeed indicator	Various inventors	Leonardo da Vinci, 1485		1900s	117
atomic cannon	Developed by the US Army	John Napier, died 1617		1950s	115
automobile	French inventor Cugnot's vehicle	Leonardo da Vinci, 1485		1769	116
	First US popular automobile	Mother Shipton, died 1561		1901	198
	Common use in the West	Andrew Jackson Davis, 1856	near future	1920s	122
	Computer-guided automobile	Arthur C. Clarke, 1958	1995		126
	End of the automobile in the West	Olaf Jonsson, 1978	1990		107
ballistic shell	Krupp weaponry works in Germany	Leonardo da Vinci, 1485		1880s	116
canal building	Caledonian Canal in Scotland	Brahan Seer, 1665		1822	64
clinometer	Used in cannon sight	Leonardo da Vinci, 1485		1600s	117
computer	First used in Allied decoder	Charles Babbage, 1819	near future	1940s	126
	Widespread industrial use	Jules Verne, 1875	near future	1960s	122
	Worldwide common use	Arthur C. Clarke, 1958	near future		124
	"Intelligent" computer	Herman Kahn, 1979	2000		149
electrocardiograph	Instituted in Europe	Jules Verne, 1875		1903	122
electronics increase	Worldwide use	Daniel Bell, 1967	2000		158
	Society based on their use	Alvin Toffler, 1971	2000		151
energy resources, depleted	In the US	Harry Harrison, 1966	1999		141
	As a result of over-consumption	The Club of Rome, 1972	2072		156
	Worldwide shortages	Jesco von Puttkamer, 1979	2000		154
energy resources, enough	Availability of ores	Herman Kahn, 1975	continuing		148
energy resources, new sources	Sea mining	Arthur C. Clarke, 1958	1990		126
	Worldwide development	Daniel Bell, 1967	2000		158
	Solar energy	Isaac Asimov, 1972	1990		126
	Waste resources	Isaac Asimov, 1972	2300		126
environment, clean	Worldwide clean-up	Herman Kahn, 1975	1985		148
environment, destroyed	As a result of nuclear war	Robert Silverberg, 1972	near future		141
	Worldwide disruption	The Club of Rome, 1972	2072		156
environment, endangered	As a result of nuclear power mis-use	Linus Pauling, 1976	2050		155
gears	Instituted by watchmakers	Leonardo da Vinci, 1485		1700s	117
hovercraft	Trans-Atlantic crossing	Arthur C. Clarke, 1958	1990		126
icebergs	Used for water supply in California	Rand Corporation, 1970s	near future		147
	Commercial use	Jeane Dixon, 1979	1985		95

jack	In all American cars	Leonardo da Vinci, 1485	1940s		117
laser	Developed in the West	Francis Bacon, died 1626	1960s		117
levitator	Individual levitating devices	Roger Bacon, died 1292			114
machine gun	Used in US Civil War	Leonardo da Vinci, 1485	1862		116
medical advancements	Worldwide advances	Arthur C. Clarke, 1958		near future	125
	Reversing aging, cancer cure, etc.	Sandra McNeil, 1978		1981-2000	104
	Bionics	F. M. Esfandiary, 1978		2000	157
military tank	"Big Willie," developed by England	Leonardo da Vinci, 1485	1915		116
nuclear accident	Three Mile Island	US Government, 1969	1979	near future	205
	Disaster due to nuclear power	Linus Pauling, 1976	1979	2000-2025	155
	In the US	Simon Alexander, 1979		late 1980s	103
parachute	Tests made by jumping from a balloon	Leonardo da Vinci, 1485	1797		117
passenger and freighter submarines	German "milk cows"	Nostradamus, 1555	1941		50
	Swiss tourist submarine	Francis Bacon, died 1626	1965		118
	Nuclear submarine	Jules Verne, 1866	1961		122
	Energy-efficient freighter submarines	Arthur C. Clarke, 1958		1990	126
plant hybrids	Tomato	Francis Bacon, died 1626	1870s		118
refrigerator	"Icebox" in the US	Francis Bacon, died 1626	1890s		118
research laboratories	In Europe and the US	Francis Bacon, died 1626	early 1900s		117
robots	In the Western world	Bulwer Lytton, 1871	1970s		132
	Used for surveillance	Harlan Ellison, 1971		2010	135
	For household use	Sandra McNeil, 1978			104
submarine warfare	In the North Atlantic	Nostradamus, 1555	1941		50
	US wooden submarine, The Turtle	Francis Bacon, 1593	1771		118
telephone	Bell's invention	Francis Bacon, died 1626	1876		117
telephone purchasing	Current experimentation	Isaac Asimov, 1972		near future	126
television	First television in England	H. G. Wells, 1895	1921		120
test-tube conception	Does away with family	Aldous Huxley, 1931		2531	139
	Worldwide implementation	F. M. Esfandiary, 1978		2000	158
train	Introduced in Ireland	St. Columbcille, 565 A.D.	1834		33
	Brought in at Inverness	Brahan Seer, 1665	1862		65
	US trans-continental link	Margaret Fuller, 1824	1862		123

A Catalogue of Doomsters

WHO THEY WERE	WHEN THEY PREDICTED THE END	WHEN IT WAS SUPPOSED TO HAPPEN
Montanus, Prisca & Maximilla	156 A.D.	near future
Book of Revelations	3rd Century A.D.	
Novatian	4th Century A.D.	
Donatus	4th Century A.D.	
John of Toledo	1186	
Dutch Anabaptists	1530	1533
Brazilian tribes	1539	
Nostradamus	1555	3797
Sabbatai Zevi	1647	1648, 1666
Woman in the Wilderness Group	1693	
Johann Jacob Zimmerman	1693	1694
Father George Rapp	1804	
Hapu	1825	
William Miller	1839	1843
North American Indian cults	1870s	
Henry Adams	1903	1950
Alexander Bedward	1920	December 31, 1920
Garner Ted Armstrong Herbert W. Armstrong	1934	1972, 1976
Bashilele cult	1935	1936
Huynh Phy So	1940	1940
Rudolfo Benavides	1961	1987-2001
Edward Elson	1972	December 25, 1973
Winnifred Barton	1976	June 13, 1976
John Strong	1977	October, 1978
Jeane Dixon	1978	4980
Roch "Moses" Thériault	1978	February 19, 1979
Criswell	1978	August 18, 1999
Jack Hills	1979	25 billion years
Jehovah's Witnesses	Various times	Various times

Bibliography

Books

Asimov, Isaac, *The Beginning of the End*, 1st edition, New York: Simon and Schuster Pocket Books, 1978.

Bell, Daniel, *Towards the Year 2000; Work in Progress*, Boston: Beacon Press, 1969.

Brian, Denis, *Jeane Dixon: The Witnesses*, 1st edition, Garden City, New York: Doubleday and Co., 1976.

Carter, Mary Ellen, *Edgar Cayce on Prophecy*, first printing, New York: Warner Books Inc., 1968.

Clark, Ella Elizabeth, *Indian Legends of Canada*, Toronto: McClelland and Stewart Ltd., 1969.

Clarke, Arthur C., *Prelude to Space,* New York; Harcourt Brace, 1970

Cornish, Edward, with members and staff of the World Future Society, *The Study of the Future*, Washington: World Future Society, 1977.

Dixon, Jeane, and Noorbergen, Rene, *Jeane Dixon: My Life and Prophecies*, New York: Bantam Books Inc., 1970.

Ebon, Martin, *Prophecy in Our Time*, New York: New American Library Inc., 1968.

Editors of *Pensee, Velikovsky Reconsidered*, New York: Warner Books Inc., 1976.

Fuller, Buckminster, *Ideas and Integrities*, 1st edition, Englewood Cliffs, New Jersey: Prentice-Hall, 1963.

Fuller, Buckminster, *Utopia or Oblivion: The Prospects for Humanity*, New York: Bantam Books, 1971.

Fuller, John G., *The Ghost of Flight 401*, New York: Berkeley Publishing, 1976.

Garrett, J.C., *Utopias in Literature since the Romantic Period*, Christchurch, New Zealand: University of Canterbury, 1968.

Garrison, Omar V., *The Encyclopaedia of Prophecy*, Seacaucus, New Jersey: Citadel Press, 1979.

Glass, Justine, *They Foresaw the Future,* New York: G.P. Putnam's and Sons, 1969.

Greenhouse, Herbert B., *Premonitions: A Leap into the Future*, New York: Bernard Geis Associates, 1971.

Holzer, Hans, *Predictions — Fact or Fallacy?* 1st edition, New York: Hawthorn Books, 1968.

Holzer, Hans, *The Prophets Speak*, Indianapolis: Bobbs-Merrill, 1971.

Is The Bible Really The Word of God? New York: Watchtower Bible and Tract Society, 1969.

Lanternari, Vittorio, *The Religions of the Oppressed*, New York: Alfred A. Knopf Inc., 1963.

Laver, James, *Nostradamus or The Future Foretold,* London: Collins, 1942.

Leoni, Edgar, *Nostradamus: Life and Literature,* 2nd edition, New York: Nosbooks, 1965.

Lewinsohn, Richard, *Prophets and Prediction*, London: Secker and Warburg, 1961.

Lindsey, Hal, with C.C. Carlson, *The Late Great Planet Earth*, 25th printing, Grand Rapids, Michigan: Zondervan Publishing House, 1972.

Mackenzie, Alexander, with foreward, commentary and conclusion by Elizabeth Sutherland, *The Prophecies of the Brahan Seer*, London: Constable and Co. Ltd., 1977. (Originally published 1877.)

Macrae, Norman, editor, *Highland Second Sight*, Dingwall, Scotland: George Souter, 1908.

Mesarovic, Mihajlo and Pestel, Eduard, *Mankind at the Turning Point*, 1st edition, New York: E.P. Dutton, 1974.

Montgomery, Ruth, *A Gift of Prophecy*, 24th printing, New York: Bantam Books Inc., 1968.

Our Incoming World Government, New York: Watchtower Bible and Tract Society, 1977.

Robb, Stewart, *Prophecies on World Events by Nostradamus*, New York: Liveright Publishing Corporation, 1961.

Roberts, Henry C., *The Complete Prophecies of Nostradamus*, 36th printing, Jericho, New York: Nostradamus, Inc., 1978.

Robinson, Theodore H., *Prophecy and the Prophets in Ancient Israel*, 2nd edition, London: Gerald Duckworth and Co. Ltd., 1953.

Russell, Eric, *Astrology and Prediction*, New York: Drake Publishers Inc., 1973.

Spraggett, Allen, *Ross Peterson, the new Edgar Cayce*, New York: Jove Publishing, 1974.

Stearn, Jess, *Edgar Cayce — The Sleeping Prophet*, 19th printing, New York: Bantam Books Inc., 1977.

Stearn, Jess, *The Door to the Future*, Garden City, New York: Doubleday and Co., 1963.

The Prophecies of Paracelsus, London: Rider and Co., 1974.

The Prophecies of St. Malachy and St. Columbcille, Gerrards Cross Bucks.: Colin Smythe Ltd., 1970.

Toth, Max, *Pyramid Prophecies*, 1st printing, New York: Warner Books Inc., 1979.

True Peace and Security, New York: Watchtower Bible and Tract Society, 1973.

Velikovsky, Immanuel, *Earth in Upheaval*, London: Sphere Books, 1973.

Wallace, Robert and editors of *Time, The World of Leonardo*, New York: Time-Life, 1975.

Wallechinsky, David, and Wallace, Irving, *The People's Almanac*, New York: Doubleday, 1975.

Wells, H.G., *The Shape of Things to Come,* London: Corgi Books, 1974.

Werner, Alice, *Myths and Legends of the Bantu*, London: Frank Cass and Co., Ltd., 1968.

Young, Bruce, *Hotel California,* North Vancouver, British Columbia: The Good Earth, 1979.

Newspapers and Magazines

Ambroziak, Alycia, "Cultists Welcome Kin, but not with Open Arms," *Montreal Star*, April 20, 1979.

Anderson, F.H., editor, *Future Report*, November 8, 1976 (published by Foundation for the Future, Newburyport, Mass.)

Colombo, John Robert, *"Who Was the Far-Sighted Centennius?"* *The Globe and Mail*, Toronto, August 11, 1979.

Dillon, Marilyn, "Man Foresaw Airline Disaster in Dreams," *Cincinnati Enquirer*, May 31, 1979.

Dixon, Jeane, "Predictions for the Eighties," *The Star*, December 25, 1979.

Esfandiary, F.M., "Optimism, Abundance, Universalism and Immortality," *The Futurist,* June, 1978.

Goodman, David, "Big Brother May Be Right on Schedule," *The Futurist*, December, 1978.

Kirk, Malcolm, "An Interview with Arthur C. Clarke," *Omni*, March, 1979.

O'Brien, Richard, producer, "The Future," broadcast on *Morningside*, CBC, June 6, 1979.

O'Neill, Gerard, "Space Colonies — The High Frontier," *The Futurist*, February, 1976.

Puttkamer, Jesco von, "The Industrialization of Space," *The Futurist*, June, 1979.

Sears, Val, "Are You Ready for the End of the World?" *Toronto Star*, December 3, 1978.

Stine, Harry G., "Industry Goes to Space," *Omni*, April, 1979.

Tarr, Leslie K., "Doomsters Prove Poor Prophets, Minister Says," *Toronto Star*, March 5, 1977.

Credits

The authors wish to thank the following sources for illustrative material:

Tony Hauser, Bantam, page 8; *William Blake: Selected Drawings,* by Carolyn Keay, Academy Editions, UK, 1975, page 14; Wide World Photos, page 23; Wide World Photos, page 24; Wide World Photos, page 26; Wide World Photos, page 27; Bord Failte Photo, page 30; *Nineteenth Century Locomotive Engravings,* William Fenton, Hugh Evelyn Publishers, from *The Railway Gazette,* page 33; CP Wirephoto, page 35; Wide World Photos, page 38; Peter Commins, after *The Complete Prophecies of Nostradamus,* translated, edited and interpreted by Henry C. Roberts, 1978, page 46; Peter Commins, after *International Portrait Gallery,* Gale Research Company, 1968, page 47; CP Picture Service, page 49; CP Picture Service, page 49; Wheeler Newspaper Syndicate, top, page 51; Emma Hesse and Peter Commins, bottom, page 51; Associated Press Photo, page 52; The British Tourist Authority, page 58; Peter Commins, after a painting by David Scougal, circa 1660, page 60; Emma Hesse and Peter Commins, page 63; The British Tourist Authority, page 64; The British Tourist Authority, page 65; Peter Commins, page 66; The British Tourist Authority, page 67; The British Tourist Authority, page 69; Association for Research and Enlightenment Foundation photo, page 74; Emma Hesse and Peter Commins, page 76; Wide World Photos, page 78; Wide World Photos, page 79; Wide World Photos, page 83; The *Toronto Globe & Mail,* page 86; Public Archives Canada, top, page 89; Wide World Photos, bottom, page 89; Wide World Photos, page 93; Wide World Photos, page 96; Courtesy Sandra McNeil, left, page 98; Hugh Wesley, *Toronto Sun,* center, page 98; Courtesy Irene Hughes, right, page 98; National Film Board of Canada, page 100; Wide World Photos, page 103; James Goodwin photo, page 108; National Archives, page 109; NASA photo, page 112; Wide World Photos, page 115; Leonardo da Vinci, in the Biblioteca

Reale, Turin, Italy, page 116; Peter Commins, after Leonardo da Vinci, in the Bibliothèque Nationale, Paris, France, page 117; Leonardo da Vinci, in the Biblioteca Reale, Turin, Italy, page 118; Peter Commins, after *The Essays of Francis Bacon,* Davies and Wrigley, 1973, left, page 119; Peter Commins, after *Cyrano de Bergerac,* Georges Mongrédien, 1964, right, page 119; Verne engraving from *Fantastic Planets,* Jean-Claude Suarès and Richard Siegal, text by David Owen, Reed Books, 1979, page 120; NASA photo, page 121; CP Photo, page 125; Peter Commins, page 126; UPI Photo, page 127; Peter Commins, page 128; National Film Board of Canada, page 130; Utopia Illustration from *Science Fiction, An Illustrated History,* Samuel J. Lundwall, Grosset & Dunlop, New York, 1977, page 131; National Archives, page 134; Wide World Photos, page 139; National Film Board of Canada, page 142; NASA photo, page 144; National Film Board of Canada, page 146; Hudson Institute photo, page 148; National Film Board of Canada, page 150; Peter Commins, after NASA, page 153; *Toronto Sun*/CP Photo, page 154; Wide World Photos, page 157; Wide World Photos, page 159; Peter Commins, page 162; Peter Commins, page 169; *Le Soleil* of Quebec City photo, page 174; Peter Commins, page 175; Keystone Press Agency Ltd., page 176; *Modern World Book of Ships,* Raymond Blackman, Low, Marston & Company, London, page 179; CP Photo, page 183; Wide World Photos, page 185; Gordon Counsell photo, CP Picture Service, page 187; Royal Ontario Museum photo, page 188; *The Prophecies of Paracelsus,* Rider, page 194; *The Prophecies of Paracelsus,* Rider, page 195; Peter Commins, page 197; *Toronto Sun,* page 201; Wide World Photos, page 206.

Permission to use copyright material is gratefully acknowledged to the following:

Toronto Sun Publishing Company, for a section of the interview with Ray Bradbury on page 8; Edgar Cayce readings © 1971 by the Edgar Cayce Foundation. Reprinted by permission in chapter 5; Victor Gollancz Ltd. and Curtis Brown Ltd. for "Against Romanticism," from *A Case of Samples,* by Kingsley Amis on page 99; Faber & Faber Ltd. for "An Eclogue for Christmas,"from *The Collected Poems of Louis MacNeice,* by Louis MacNeice on page 129.

Although every effort has been made to ensure that permissions for all material were obtained, those sources not formally acknowledged here will be included in all future editions of this book.